Flow

Flower Color Guide

Taylor and Michael Putnam

On Color   6

Flowers   15

Appendices   417
Before You Shop   419
Basic Flower Care   421
Essential Tools   425
Preparing Vessels   429
Suggested Color Palettes   431
Notes on Sustainability   433
Tear-out Flower Chips   437

Index of botanical names   477
Index of common names   481

On Color

Color is the aspect that most defines our work at Putnam & Putnam, whether it's for arranging flowers or creating large-scale floral installations. We love color, and we think it creates the best visual stories.

We create our floral designs from intuition. Color is a narrative, and we let the color of flowers guide us, layering with them for depth. We use all colors, from dustier antique shades to vibrant saturated varieties. We use flowers and foliage as well as other elements such as fruit and vines to give our arrangements a sense of looseness and an old-world feeling—although we're very "flower-heavy" rather than "greens-heavy".

Michael has the most sophisticated eye for color, developed since his childhood in southern California, growing up appreciating flowers and gardens, then further advanced when he was studying interior design and working in that field. Taylor comes to her knowledge of color through her career as a photographer.

We start our designs with a color in mind, and then we pore through the flower market on West 28th Street in New York City, where we live, in early morning searches to find all the flowers that will help tell our color story that day. It's always the thought of a color that leads and inspires us, and this is the book we wish we'd had to help guide us when we started Putnam & Putnam in 2014.

This is an easy-to-use reference book about flower types, the spectrum of colors they grow in, and the seasons in which they are available. Think of it as an essential primer for flower arranging and selection, whether it's flowers for your home, to give as a present, or for a dinner party or wedding.

We emphasize seasonality enthusiastically. You can now get many varieties anywhere, anytime. The flower market is global, with flowers flown all over the world in all seasons and mostly passing through Holland. The main goal for us, however—and probably for you, too, if you are reading this book—in addition to rightsizing our global footprint, is to use the freshest, most interesting and beautiful flowers at hand. The most beautiful flowers you will find are usually those that are in season near your home, at the peak of their growing season. Not only will this make them the most beautiful, but also the most affordable because they do not have to be transported from a great distance and they will last longer.

The problem for beginners, which we most certainly once were, is that most people don't grow up knowing a lot about flowers. Almost every time we meet with new clients—very often brides planning their weddings—the first thing they say to us is, "I don't know any of the names of flowers but I do know that I love..." and usually it's peonies and garden roses. Or they say, "I love pink flowers," or another color, "but I don't know what types they are."

As Putnam & Putnam developed its vocabulary as a business, we also realized we wanted to become a resource for people to learn as much as they cared to learn about flowers, not just flower arranging. With cooking, the more you know about food and how different ingredients go together, the more your appreciation of food preparation expands and with that your cooking skills grow as well. It's the same with flowers. The more you know about them, the more vibrant your experience and knowledge of using them becomes, and it gets better and better with more time and more experience. And from a consumer's point of view, you're much more informed when you go shopping for flowers or work with florists.

The history of flower arranging is the story of changing trends and styles in terms of what is popular. We like to create a romantic and loose feeling, with lush and faded colors, aiming for gesture, texture, things spilling out and falling onto the table.

We believe in gradating colors of flowers, moving away from arranging flowers in what we see as a contrived, polka-dot way without using enough transitional or blending colors. It elevates your floral design to become more aware of the colors in between. When we teach flower-arranging workshops around the world—one of our favorite things to do—we focus on the appreciation of gradating colors. Our classes usually begin with having two stems representing two colors from different sides of the spectrum and then adding stems of different colors that bring the arrangement together. It's fascinating to see how the colors completely change and morph into each other when you work this way.

Different flowers bring different qualities to an arrangement, and we believe that it's important to include a balance of these qualities. We think of flowers in four groups: face flowers, textural flowers, gestural stems, and fillers. Face flowers, such as amaryllis, peonies, or dahlias, provide the main feature or big statement; textural flowers, such as astilbe, wax flower, and andromeda, add complexity; gestural stems, such as foxgloves, fritillaria, and tulips, create shape, depth, and movement; and fillers, such as roses, lisianthus, and carnations, are useful for blending colors and creating a base structure.

What's the best way to use this book? We suggest that you begin with the colors that you like best, turn to those pages and see which of those flowers will be in season when you will be using them. People get really sold on having to have specific flower types and a specific color. While you turn the pages of this book, we hope that you discover colors and flowers types that you maybe hadn't thought of before, and explore further by using our suggestions of what colors go nicely together.

Preparation is really the key to a successful floral scheme. So have in mind an image of what you are looking for before you go to your florist shop or flower market. Know the occasion for which you are shopping. Is it flowers for a wedding, a birthday or dinner party, or flowers for you to enjoy home alone? Know the season. The flowers that you find available locally now will be the most affordable, freshest, and will last longer. And remember that there's more to a flower than just its face. Stems have amazing shapes, leaves too, and every flower has a movement.

At first we thought we should organize this book by season. Then we thought we should organize it alphabetically by the name and type of flower. Ultimately we decided to organize it by color as we've observed that color is how people instinctively think about flowers—color first. You'll find the colors gradated from the light-colored flowers—whites, creams, and pale pastels—to the darker flowers in the rich color palette of purples, browns, and almost blacks.

We've included 400 flowers. You can imagine that choosing the flowers was an adventure, a very creative endeavor. There are so many different flowers that we could have done a book with just 400 tulips. Hopefully we've included your favorites. We wanted to find the best, fullest range of colors and we spent a year photographing seasonally from autumn onward into spring and summer.

We met in 2008 when we were college students in southern California while in line shopping at a grocery store. Taylor was studying photography and Michael interior design. Our partnership began, and we knew from the start that we wanted to work together someday, but we just didn't have a clue how.

We moved to New York City when Michael was accepted at the interior design program at the Fashion Institute of Technology. Taylor got a job doing photo-retouching and pursued her photography career on weekends. After F.I.T., Michael began working in a design firm and quickly realized his new profession was not tactile enough for him. As a hobby, he began to arrange flowers from the farmers' market and local parks on the weekend. Taylor photographed them as small still lifes and posted them to Instagram. People quickly took notice and started to ask if Michael would do things for friends, dinner parties and bridal showers—small things like that. Everything changed when *Vogue* magazine reached out and asked if Michael would do flowers for an editorial story. After that story posted on the magazine's website, it all snowballed from there.

Soon after, we had enough work for us to quit our day jobs, move to Manhattan and start Putnam & Putnam. We first started in a small apartment on the Lower East Side, and we have now moved to the heart of New York's flower district on West 28th Street.

As Putnam & Putnam grows and develops, we continue to learn more about the flowers that we work with, to discover beautiful new ones, and be amazed by the creative potential in every stem.

"Do what you please, follow your own star; be original if you want to be and don't if you don't want to be," Constance Spry said about flower arranging. "Just be natural and light-hearted and pretty and simple and overflowing and baroque and bare and austere and stylized and wild and daring and conservative, and learn and learn and learn," she said. "Open your mind to every form of beauty."

How to use this book

Use the captions to identify the flowers, know what category of flower to treat them as in an arrangement, and find out the time of year they are at their best at the market.

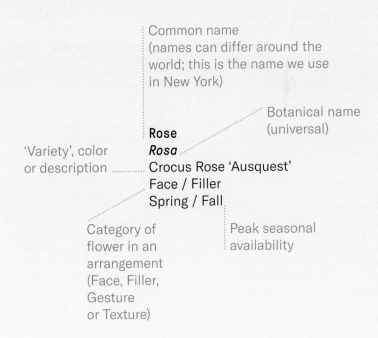

Common name
(names can differ around the world; this is the name we use in New York)

Botanical name
(universal)

'Variety', color or description

Rose
Rosa
Crocus Rose 'Ausquest'
Face / Filler
Spring / Fall

Category of flower in an arrangement (Face, Filler, Gesture or Texture)

Peak seasonal availability

Flowers

Azalea
Rhododendron molle
White
Filler
Spring

Cyclamen
Cyclamen persicum
White
Filler
Spring

Hydrangea
Hydrangea macrophylla
White
Filler
Year-round

Tweedia
Tweedia caerulea
'Pint White'
Filler
Year-round

Flowering cherry
Prunus x *subhirtella*
'Autumnalis' white
Gesture / Filler
Spring

Kangaroo paw
Anigozanthos
'Bush Diamond'
Gesture / Texture
Year-round

Stock
Matthiola incana
Double white
Gesture / Filler
Year-round

Ranunculus
Ranunculus asiaticus
Double white
Face / Filler
Winter / Spring

Flannel flower
Actinotus helianthi
White
Filler / Texture
Winter / Spring

Delphinium
Delphinium
'Centurion White'
Face / Gesture
Year-round

Paper white
Narcissus papyraceus
White
Filler
Winter / Spring

Rose
Rosa
'Tibet'
Filler
Year-round

Allium / Naples onion
Allium neapolitanum
White
Gesture / Texture
Spring / Summer

Lily
Lilium
'Premium Blond'
Face
Year-round

Spray carnation
Dianthus
'Grenadin White'
Texture / Filler
Year-round

Scabiosa
Scabiosa columbaria
White
Gesture
Year-round

Nerine
Nerine bowdenii
'Pallida' white
Filler / Texture
Year-round

Anemone
Anemone coronaria
Single white
Face
Winter / Spring

Spirea
Spiraea
'Arguta'
Gesture / Texture
Winter / Spring

Anemone
Anemone
De Caen Group white
Face
Winter / Spring

Rose
Rosa
Winchester Cathedral 'Auscat'
Face / Filler
Spring / Fall

Rose
Rosa
'White Majolica'
Filler
Year-round

Spray carnation
Dianthus
'Star Snow Tessino'
Filler / Texture
Year-round

Peony
Paeonia
'Bowl of Cream'
Face
Spring

Amaryllis
Hippeastrum
'White Dazzler'
Face
Winter

Calla lily
Zantedeschia aethiopica
White
Face / Gesture
Year-round

Astrantia
Astrantia major
'White Giant'
Texture / Filler
Year-round

Lilac
Syringa vulgaris
White
Filler
Spring

Dahlia
Dahlia
'Blizzard'
Face
Summer / Fall

Gladiolus
Gladiolus x *colvillii*
'Albus'
Gesture
Summer / Fall

Gladiolus
Gladiolus
'White Prosperity'
Gesture
Year-round

Freesia
Freesia
White
Filler
Year-round

Narcissus
Narcissus poeticus hybrid
White
Face / Filler
Winter / Spring

Tulip
Tulipa
'White Liberstar'
Gesture
Spring

Hyacinth
Hyacinthus orientalis
White
Filler
Winter / Spring

Rose
Rosa
'Garden Snow'
Filler
Year-round

Lily of the valley
Convallaria majalis
White
Texture
Spring

Solomon's Seal
Polygonatum biflorum
White
Gesture
Spring

Muscari
Muscari azureum
'Album'
Texture / Filler
Winter / Spring

Gooseneck loosestrife
Lysimachia clethroides
White
Gesture
Summer

Lisianthus
Eustoma russellianum
White
Filler
Year-round

Gerbera daisy
Gerbera x *hybrida*
White
Face / Gesture
Year-round

Sweet pea
Lathyrus odoratus
White
Texture / Filler / Gesture
Winter / Spring

Snowflake
Leucojum aestivum
White
Texture
Winter

Everlasting pea
Lathyrus latifolius
'Albus' white
Texture / Filler / Gesture
Winter / Spring

Astilbe
Astilbe
'Deutschland'
Texture
Year-round

Gladiolus
Gladiolus
'The Bride'
Gesture / Filler
Summer

Tulip
Tulipa
'Honeymoon'
Gesture
Spring

Calla lily
Zantedeschia
'Aspen'
Gesture
Year-round

Anthurium
Anthurium
'Acropolis'
Face
Year-round

Dahlia
Dahlia
'Figaro' white
Face
Summer / Fall

Cosmos
Cosmos bipinnatus
Double white
Gesture
Summer

Nigella
Nigella damascena
White
Texture
Spring / Summer

Blue lace flower
Trachymene coerulea
'Lacy Pink'
Gesture
Spring / Summer

Peony
Paeonia lactiflora
'Festiva Maxima'
Face
Spring

Anthurium
Anthurium
'Lumina'
Face
Year-round

Quince
Chaenomeles speciosa
'Nivalis' white
Gesture
Winter

Wax flower
Chamelaucium uncinatum
White
Texture / Filler
Year-round

Heath rice flower
Pimelea phylicoides
White
Texture
Spring / Summer

Spirea
Spiraea thunbergii
White
Gesture / Texture
Winter / Spring

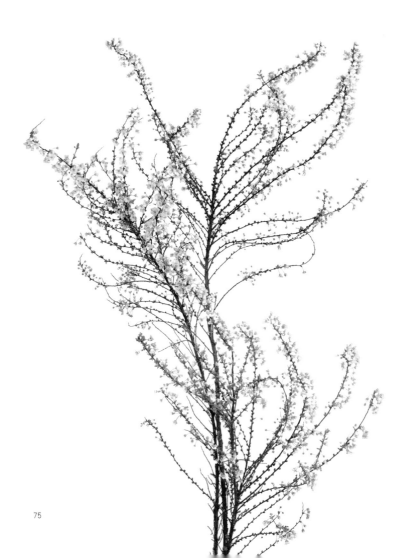

Peony
Paeonia lactiflora
'Sonata'
Face
Spring

Peony
Paeonia lactiflora
'Rooster Reveille'
Face
Spring

Sweet pea
Lathyrus odoratus
Pale pink
Texture / Filler / Gesture
Winter / Spring

Peony
Paeonia lactiflora
'Duchesse de Nemours'
Face
Spring

Butterfly ranunculus
Ranunculus asiaticus
'Butterfly Lux' cream
Gesture / Filler
Winter / Spring

Oncidium orchid
Oncidium hybrid
White and pink
Texture / Gesture
Year-round

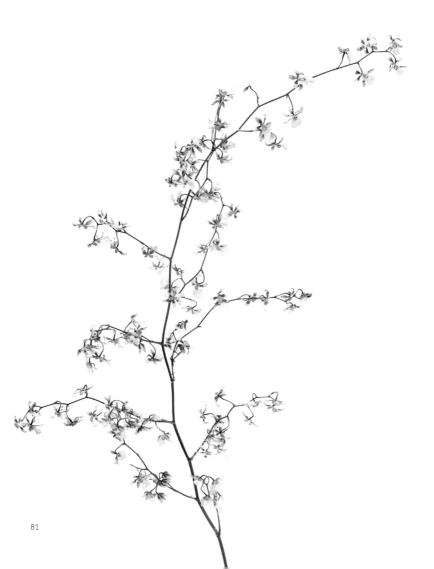

Dogwood
Cornus kousa
var. *chinensis*
Gesture / Filler
Spring

Foxglove
Digitalis purpurea
f. albiflora
Gesture / Face
Spring / Summer

Rose
Rosa
'Champagne'
Filler
Year-round

Rose
Rosa
'Charity'
Filler
Spring / Fall

Jasmine
Jasminum polyanthum
White and pink
Texture
Winter / Spring

Narcissus
Narcissus
'Salome'
Face / Filler
Spring

Lily
Lilium
Pink roselily
Face
Year-round

Stock
Matthiola incana
Double peach
Filler / Gesture
Year-round

Astilbe
Astilbe
'Elizabeth Bloom'
Texture
Year-round

Hyacinth
Hyacinthus orientalis
Pale pink
Filler
Winter / Spring

Dahlia
Dahlia
'Cream and Pink'
Face
Summer / Fall

Chrysanthemum
Chrysanthemum
'Seaton's Je Dore'
Face
Fall

Epidendrum
Epidendrum hybrid
Pale pink
Gesture
Year-round

Rose
Rosa
'Sahara'
Filler
Year-round

Tulip
Tulipa
'Apricot Beauty'
Gesture
Spring

Bearded iris
Iris germanica
'Party Dress'
Face
Spring

Statice
Limonium sinuatum
Peach
Texture
Year-round

Pansy
Viola hybrid
Pale pink and yellow
Filler
Winter / Spring

Rose
Rosa
'Cappuccino'
Filler
Year-round

Stock
Matthiola incana
Single petal peach
Gesture / Filler
Year-round

Rose
Rosa
'Sahara Sensation'
Filler
Year-round

Carnation
Dianthus
Nude
Filler
Year-round

Dahlia
Dahlia
'Cafe au Lait'
Face
Summer / Fall

Rose
Rosa
Juliet 'Ausjameson'
Face / Filler
Year-round

Lisianthus
Eustoma russellianum
Peach
Filler
Year-round

Lily
Lilium
Peach
Face
Year-round

Rose
Rosa
'Emily'
Filler
Year-round

Rose
Rosa
'Pink Majolica'
Filler
Year-round

Dogwood
Cornus kousa
Pink
Gesture / Filler
Spring

Tree peony
Paeonia x *suffruticosa*
'Kopper Kettle'
Face
Spring

Rose
Rosa
'Distant Drum'
Face / Filler
Spring / Fall

Gerbera daisy
Gerbera x *hybrida*
Apricot
Face / Gesture
Year-round

Ranunculus
Ranunculus asiaticus
Double peach
Face / Filler
Winter / Spring

Rose
Rosa
Pink-peach
Face / Filler
Spring / Fall

Phalaenopsis orchid
Phalaenopsis hybrid
Pale yellow and pink
Face / Filler / Gesture
Year-round

Parrot tulip
Tulipa
'Libretto Parrot'
Gesture
Spring

Rose
Rosa
'Quicksand'
Filler
Year-round

Calla lily
Zantedeschia
'Kiwi Blush'
Gesture
Year-round

Ranunculus
Ranunculus asiaticus
Double pink
Face / Filler
Winter / Spring

Foxglove
Digitalis purpurea
Pale pink
Gesture / Face
Spring / Summer

Rose
Rosa
'Secret Garden'
Filler
Year-round

Peony
Paeonia lactiflora
'Lady Gay'
Face
Spring

Rose
Rosa
'Pink Raddish'
Texture / Filler
Year-round

Carnation
Dianthus
Variegated
Filler
Year-round

Rose
Rosa
'Caffe Latte'
Face / Filler
Year-round

Coxcomb
Celosia cristata
Green and pale pink
Filler
Summer / Fall

Rose
Rosa
'Amnesia'
Filler
Year-round

Celosia
Celosia spicata
Pink-purple
Gesture / Texture
Summer / Fall

Yarrow
Achillea millefolium
Pink-purple
Filler / Texture
Year-round

Lilac
Syringa vulgaris
'Beauty of Moscow'
Filler
Spring

Tuberose
Polianthes tuberosa
'Pink Sapphire'
Gesture
Year-round

Cherry blossom
Prunus glandulosa
'Sinensis' double pink
Gesture / Filler
Spring

Larkspur
Consolida regalis
Pale pink
Filler / Texture
Year-round

Sweet pea
Lathyrus odoratus
Lavender
Texture / Filler / Gesture
Winter / Spring

Campanula / bellflower
Campanula medium
Pale blue
Filler
Spring / Summer

Scabiosa
Scabiosa caucasica
Pale blue
Gesture
Year-round

Statice
Limonium sinuatum
Pale blue
Filler
Year-round

Agapanthus
Agapanthus praecox
Blue
Texture / Filler
Year-round

Nigella
Nigella damascena
Blue
Texture
Spring / Summer

Blue Star
Amsonia tabernaemontana
Blue
Texture / Filler
Summer

Allium
Allium cepa
'Snake Ball'
Gesture
Spring

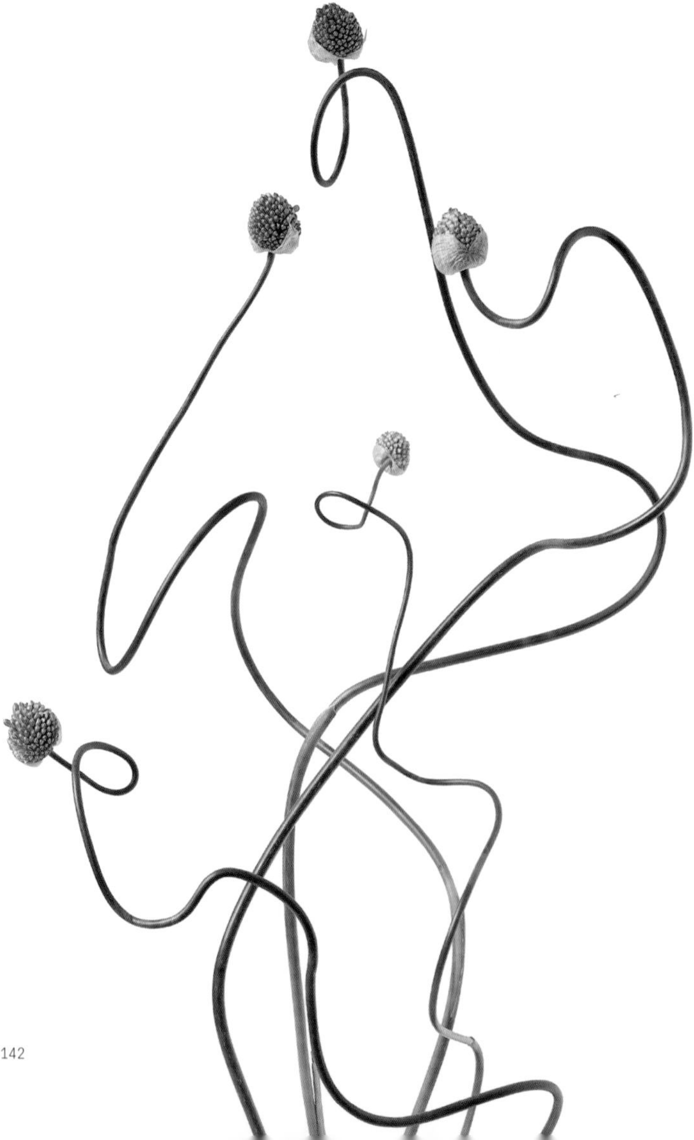

Fritilaria
Fritillaria hermonis
Green and brown
Gesture
Spring

Coxcomb
Celosia cristata
Pale green
Filler
Summer / Fall

Fritillaria
Fritillaria pontica
Green and brown
Gesture
Spring

Hellebore
Helleborus x *hybridus*
Double green and purple
Face / Filler
Winter / Spring

Fritillaria
Fritillaria persica
'Ivory Bells'
Face / Gesture
Spring

Hellebore
Helleborus x *hybridus*
Green and cream
Face / Filler
Winter / Spring

Tuberose
Polianthes tuberosa
'The Pearl'
Gesture
Year-round

Tulip
Tulipa
'White Parrot'
Gesture
Spring

Vibernum
Viburnum opulus
'Roseum'
Filler
Spring

Ranunculus
Ranunculus asiaticus
Double green
Face / Filler
Winter / Spring

French parrot tulip
Tulipa
Green
Gesture
Spring

Hellebore
Helleborus x *hybridus*
Green and purple
Face / Filler
Winter / Spring

Allium / Sicilian onion
Allium siculum
Cream and brown
Texture
Spring

Andromeda
Pieris japonica
White
Texture / Filler
Winter / Spring

Queen Anne's lace
Daucus carota
'Dara'
Gesture / Texture
Summer / Fall

Hellebore / Christmas rose
Helleborus niger
Brown
Face / Filler
Winter / Spring

Hydrangea
Hydrangea macrophylla
Brown and pink
Filler
Year-round

Foxtail Lily
Eremurus robustus
Peach
Gesture
Spring / Summer

Rose
Rosa
'Koko Loko'
Face / Filler
Spring / Fall

Wax flower
Chamelaucium uncinatum
Pink and white variegated
Texture / Filler
Year-round

Kangaroo paw
Anigozanthos
Pink and orange
Texture
Year-round

Ranunculus
Ranunculus asiaticus
Double white and brown
Face / Filler
Winter / Spring

Snake's head fritillary
Fritillaria meleagris
Purple
Gesture / Texture
Spring

Grevillea
Grevillea pteridifolia
Pale yellow
Gesture / Texture
Year-round

Rose
Rosa
'Golden Mustard'
Filler
Year-round

Scabiosa
Scabiosa atropurpurea
Pale cream
Gesture
Year-round

Chamomile
Matricaria chamomilla
White and yellow
Texture / Filler
Year-round

Narcissus
Narcissus
'Bridal Crown'
Filler
Winter / Spring

Easter lily
Lilium longiflorum
White
Face
Year-round

Peony
Paeonia lactiflora
'Day Star'
Face
Spring

Daisy mum
Chrysanthemum
Hybrid yellow
Filler
Year-round

Lady's slipper orchid
Paphiopedilum
Yellow
Face
Year-round

Rose
Rosa
Crocus Rose 'Ausquest'
Face / Filler
Spring / Fall

Peony
Paeonia lactiflora
'Claire de Lune'
Face
Spring

Peony
Paeonia lactiflora
'Lemon Dream'
Face
Spring

Narcissus
Narcissus
'Tahiti'
Gesture / Filler
Spring

Gloriosa lily
Gloriosa superba
'Lutea'
Texture / Gesture
Year-round

Forsythia
Forsythia x intermedia
Yellow
Gesture / Texture
Spring

Pansy
Viola hybrid
Yellow
Filler
Winter / Spring

Tulip
Tulipa
'Yellow Flight'
Gesture
Spring

Freesia
Freesia
Double yellow
Filler
Year-round

Tulip
Tulipa
'Monte Spider'
Gesture
Spring

Gerbera daisy
Gerbera x hybrida
Butter yellow
Face
Year-round

Butterfly ranunculus
Ranunculus asiaticus
Yellow
Gesture / Filler
Winter / Spring

French parrot tulip
Tulipa
Yellow
Gesture
Spring

Witch hazel
Hamamelis x *intermedia*
Yellow
Gesture / Texture
Winter / Spring

Oncidium orchid
Oncidium
Hybrid yellow
Filler / Gesture
Year-round

Goldenrod
Solidago canadensis
Yellow
Filler / Texture
Summer / Fall

Mimosa
Acacia retinodes
Yellow
Filler / Texture
Winter / Spring

Narcissus
Narcissus
'Soleil d'Or'
Filler
Winter / Spring

Daffodil
Narcissus pseudonarcissus
Yellow
Face
Winter / Spring

Yarrow
Achillea filipendulina
Gold
Filler / Texture
Year-round

Calendula
Calendula officinalis
Yellow
Filler
Spring / Summer

Ranunculus
Ranunculus asiaticus
Clooney series, double yellow
Face / Filler
Winter / Spring

French marigold
Tagetes patula
Striped mix
Texture / Gesture
Summer

French tulip
Tulipa
Yellow and red
Gesture
Spring

Oncidium orchid
Oncidium
Yellow
Gesture / Texture
Year-round

Coxcomb
Celosia cristata
Yellow
Filler
Summer / Fall

Sweet pea
Lathyrus odoratus
Yellow dyed
Texture / Filler / Gesture
Winter / Spring

Lady's slipper orchid
Paphiopedilum hybrid
Brown and green
Face
Year-round

Lily
Lilium
'Solange'
Face
Year-round

Rose
Rosa
'Combo'
Filler
Year-round

Butterfly ranunculus
Ranunculus asiaticus
Single orange
Gesture / Filler
Winter / Spring

Golden lantern lily
Sandersonia aurantiaca
Orange
Gesture / Texture
Spring / Summer

Calendula
Calendula officinalis
'Indian Prince'
Filler
Spring / Summer

Dahlia
Dahlia
'Lakeview Lucky'
Face / Filler
Summer / Fall

Butterfly weed
Asclepias tuberosa
Orange
Filler / Texture
Year-round

Gloriosa lily
Gloriosa superba
Orange
Gesture
Year-round

Narcissus
Narcissus
'Johann Strauss'
Filler
Spring

Birds of Paradise
Strelitzia reginae
Orange
Face / Gesture
Year-round

Ranunculus
Ranunculus asiaticus
Gold and red variegated
Face / Filler
Winter / Spring

Pincushion protea
Leucospermum
'Carnival Orange'
Face / Texture
Year-round

Epidendrum
Epidendrum hybrid
Orange
Face / Gesture
Year-round

Ranunculus
Ranunculus asiaticus
Double orange
Face / Filler
Winter / Spring

Orange chincherinchee
Ornithogalum dubium
Orange
Filler
Year-round

Fritillaria
Fritillaria imperialis
Orange
Face / Gesture
Spring

Icelandic poppy
Papaver nudicaule
Peach
Face / Gesture
Winter / Spring

Rose
Rosa
Renaissance series 'Claire'
Face / Filler
Spring / Fall

Ranunculus
Ranunculus asiaticus
Clooney series, peach
Face / Filler
Winter / Spring

Gomphrena
Gomphrena globosa
Orange
Filler
Summer / Fall

Anthurium
Anthurium
'Rothschildianum'
Face
Year-round

Calla lily
Zantedeschia
'Mango'
Gesture / Filler
Year-round

Martagon hybrid
Lilium x *martagon*
'Orange Marmalade'
Gesture / Texture
Summer

French tulip
Tulipa
'Flaming Parrot'
Gesture
Spring

Dahlia
Dahlia
'Iced Tea'
Face / Filler
Summer / Fall

Icelandic poppy
Papaver nudicaule
Orange
Gesture / Face
Winter / Spring

Heliconia
Heliconia stricta
Red
Face
Year-round

Plumosa celosia
Celosia argentea
Rust
Filler / Texture
Summer / Fall

Tulip
Tulipa
'Leo'
Gesture
Spring

Spider mum
Chrysanthemum
Orange and yellow
Face / Filler
Fall

Rose
Rosa
'Toffee'
Filler
Year-round

Anthurium
Anthurium
'Hawaii'
Face
Year-round

Coxcomb
Celosia cristata
Rust
Filler
Summer / Fall

Spider mum
Chrysanthemum
'Seaton's Toffee'
Face / Filler
Fall

Oncidium orchid
Oncidium hybrid
Orange and brown
Gesture / Texture
Year-round

James Story orchid
Oncidium hybrid
Yellow and brown
Gesture / Texture
Year-round

Amaryllis
Hippeastrum cybister
'Tarantula'
Face
Winter

Pitcher plant
Sarracenia leucophylla
Red and white variegated
Texture
Spring / Summer

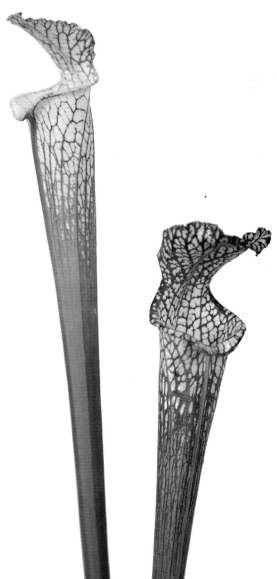

Sweet pea
Lathyrus odoratus
Brown dyed
Texture / Filler / Gesture
Winter / Spring

Ranunculus
Ranunculus asiaticus
'Charlotte' peach
Face
Winter / Spring

Beared iris
Iris germanica
Purple and brown
Face
Spring

Dahlia
Dahlia
'Bahama Apricot'
Face
Summer / Fall

Dahlia
Dahlia
'Cornel Bronze'
Face / Filler
Summer / Fall

Dahlia
Dahlia
'Gitts Crazy'
Face
Summer / Fall

Anthurium
Anthurium
'Cognac'
Face
Year-round

Tree Peony
Paeonia x *suffruticosa*
'Callie's Memory'
Face
Spring

Rose
Rosa
'Kahala'
Filler
Year-round

Amaryllis
Hippeastrum
'Rilona'
Face
Winter

Quince
Chaenomeles speciosa
Red
Gesture
Winter / Spring

Zinnia
Zinnia elegans
Coral
Face / Filler
Summer

Quince
Chaenomeles japonica
Coral
Gesture
Winter / Spring

Icelandic poppy
Papaver nudicaule
Watermelon
Face / Gesture
Winter / Spring

Dahlia
Dahlia
'Amber Queen'
Face / Filler
Summer / Fall

Christmas Bush
Ceratopetalum gummiferum
'Albery's Red'
Texture / Filler
Fall / Winter

Dahlia
Dahlia
Pale red
Face / Filler
Summer / Fall

Carnation
Dianthus
Pink and red
Filler
Year-round

Cosmos
Cosmos atrosanguineus
Dark red
Gesture
Summer / Fall

Butterfly ranunculus
Ranunculus asiaticus
Double rust
Gesture / Filler
Winter / Spring

Dahlia
Dahlia
'Red and White Fubuki'
Face
Summer / Fall

French tulip
Tulipa
'Kingsblood'
Gesture
Spring

Heliconia
Heliconia vellerigera
'King Kong'
Face
Year-round

Amaryllis
Hippeastrum
'Simply Red'
Face
Winter

266

Gerbera daisy
Gerbera x *hybrida*
Red
Face
Year-round

Anthurium
Anthurium andraeanum
Red
Face
Year-round

Cyclamen
Cyclamen persicum
Red
Filler
Spring

French parrot tulip
Tulipa
'Red Parrot'
Gesture
Spring

Spray carnation
Dianthus
'Solomio Amos'
Texture / Filler
Year-round

Zinnia
Zinnia elegans
Double red
Face / Filler
Summer

Anemone
Anemone coronaria
Red
Face
Winter / Spring

Ranunculus
Ranunculus asiaticus
Dark red
Face / Filler
Winter / Spring

Coxcomb
Celosia cristata
Dark red
Filler
Summer / Fall

Rose
Rosa
'Red Piano'
Face / Filler
Year-round

Dahlia
Dahlia
Dark red
Face
Summer / Fall

Rose
Rosa
Black Magic 'Tankalcig'
Filler
Year-round

Tulip
Tulipa
'Black Hero'
Gesture
Spring

Ranunculus
Ranunculus asiaticus
Red and brown variegated
Face / Filler
Winter / Spring

Peony
Paeonia lactiflora
'Black Swan'
Face
Spring

Peony
Paeonia lactiflora
'Chocolate Soldier'
Face
Spring

Straw flower
Xerochrysum bracteatum
Burgundy
Filler / Texture
Summer / Fall

Astilbe
Astilbe
'Red Sentinel'
Texture
Year-round

Hydrangea
Hydrangea macrophylla
Dark pink
Filler
Year-round

Cymbidium orchid
Cymbidium hybrid
Dark pink
Face / Gesture
Year-round

Lisianthus
Eustoma russellianum
Brown and purple variegated
Filler
Year-round

Tree peony
Paeonia x *suffruticosa*
Dark pink and peach
Face
Spring

Ranunculus
Ranunculus asiaticus
Dark pink
Face / Filler
Winter / Spring

Anenome
Anemone coronaria
Red and white variegated
Face
Winter / Spring

Dahlia
Dahlia
'Sonic Bloom'
Face
Summer / Fall

Ginger
Alpinia purpurata
Red
Face
Year-round

Sweet pea
Lathyrus odoratus
Red
Texture / Filler / Gesture
Winter / Spring

Azalea
Rhododendron molle
Pink hybrid
Filler
Spring

Rose
Rosa
'Pink Piano'
Face / Filler
Year-round

Rose
Rosa
Kate 'Auschris'
Face / Filler
Spring / Fall

Rose
Rosa
'Pink Floyd'
Filler
Year-round

Sweet pea
Lathyrus odoratus
Coral
Texture / Filler / Gesture
Winter / Spring

Ranunculus
Ranunculus asiaticus
Double pink and green
Face / Filler
Winter / Spring

Peony
Paeonia
'Coral Charm'
Face
Spring

Rose
Rosa
Benjamin Britten 'Ausencart'
Face / Filler
Spring / Fall

Waratah
Telopea speciosissima
Pink
Face / Texture
Summer / Fall

Rose
Rosa
'Romantic Antike'
Face / Filler
Year-round

Anthurium
Anthurium
'Marea'
Face
Year-round

Peony
Paeonia lactiflora
'Dr Alexander Fleming'
Face
Spring

Rose
Rosa
'Lady Moon'
Filler
Year-round

Ranunculus
Ranunculus asiaticus
Double pink
Face / Filler
Winter / Spring

French tulip
Tulipa
Pink
Gesture
Spring

Lisianthus
Eustoma russellianum
Double pink
Filler
Year-round

Statice
Limonium sinuatum
Pink
Filler
Year-round

Bleeding heart
Lamprocapnos spectabilis
Pink
Gesture / Texture
Spring

Dahlia
Dahlia
'Lagoon'
Face
Summer / Fall

Peony
Paeonia lactiflora
'Nymphe'
Face
Spring

Ranunculus
Ranunculus asiaticus
'Charlotte' burgundy and white
Face
Winter / Spring

Water lily
Nymphaea
Pink
Face
Year-round

Echinacea
Echinacea purpurea
Pink
Face / Filler
Summer

Scabiosa
Scabiosa columbaria
Pink
Gesture
Year-round

Peony
Paeonia lactiflora
'Sarah Bernhardt'
Face
Spring

Ranunculus
Ranunculus asiaticus
Clooney series, pale pink
Face / Filler
Winter / Spring

Plum blossom
Prunus mume
Pink
Gesture
Spring

Magnolia
Magnolia x *soulangeana*
'Alexandrina'
Face / Gesture
Spring

Rose
Rosa
'Royal Amethyst'
Face / Filler
Spring / Fall

Anemone
Anemone coronaria
Double magenta
Face
Winter / Spring

Sedum
Hylotelephium telephium
Pink
Filler
Summer / Fall

Autumn anemone / Japanese anemone
Anemone hupehensis
Pale purple
Gesture
Fall

Gerbera Daisy
Gerbera x *hybrida*
Double dark pink
Face
Year-round

Hellebore
Helleborus x *hybridus*
Dark pink
Face / Filler
Winter

Zinnia
Zinnia elegans
'Queen Lime Blush'
Filler
Summer

Grevillea
Grevillea
'Robyn Gordon'
Gesture / Texture
Year-round

Foxglove
Digitalis purpurea
Purple
Gesture / Face
Spring / Summer

Sweet pea
Lathyrus odoratus
Purple and white variegated
Texture / Filler / Gesture
Winter / Spring

Heather
Calluna vulgaris
Dark pink
Texture / Filler
Year-round

Dahlia
Dahlia
'Koko Puff'
Face / Filler
Summer / Fall

Boronia
Boronia heterophylla
Purple
Filler / Texture
Spring

Sweet William catchfly
Silene armeria
Purple
Texture / Filler
Spring

Anthurium
Anthurium
'Previa'
Face
Year-round

Dahlia
Dahlia
'Mikayla Miranda'
Face
Summer / Fall

Chrysanthemum
Chrysanthemum
Lilac
Filler
Year-round

Rose
Rosa
'Menta'
Filler
Year-round

Sweet pea
Lathyrus odoratus
'Matucana'
Texture / Filler / Gesture
Winter / Spring

Delphinium
Delphinium
Lavender
Gesture / Face
Year-round

Liatris
Liatris spicata
Purple
Gesture
Year-round

Ranunculus
Ranunculus asiaticus
Purple and mauve variegated
Face / Filler
Winter / Spring

Astrantia
Astrantia major
'Rosensinfonie'
Texture / Filler
Year-round

Bearded iris
Iris germanica
'Indian Chief'
Face
Spring

Sweet pea
Lathyrus odoratus
Chocolate dyed
Texture / Filler / Gesture
Winter / Spring

Lisianthus
Eustoma russellianum
Dark purple
Filler
Year-round

Hellebore
Helleborus x *hybridus*
Dark purple
Face / Filler
Winter / Spring

Allium
Allium cepa
Purple and gray
Gesture
Spring

Lilac
Syringa
Lavender
Texture / Filler
Spring

Oncidium orchid
Oncidium hybrid
'Kauai'
Gesture
Year-round

Sweet pea
Lathyrus odoratus
'Chocolate Flake'
Texture / Filler / Gesture
Winter / Spring

Lupine
Lupinus x *regalis*
Blue
Gesture
Spring / Summer

Clematis
Clematis alpina
'Tage Lundell' lavender
Gesture / Filler
Year-round

Hellebore
Helleborus x *hybridus*
Double pink and white variegated
Face / Filler
Winter / Spring

Bell clematis
Clematis
'Rooguchi' purple
Gesture
Spring

Kangaroo paw
Anigozanthos flavidus
'Ember' purple variegated
Gesture / Texture
Year-round

Sweet pea
Lathyrus nervosus
Purple
Texture / Filler / Gesture
Winter / Spring

Bell clematis
Clematis
'Rooguchi' blue
Gesture
Spring

Cineraria
Pericallis x *hybrida*
Blue
Texture / Filler
Spring

Water lily
Nymphaea nouchali
Lavender
Face
Year-round

Anemone
Anemone coronaria
Lavender
Face
Winter / Spring

Floss flower
Ageratum houstonianum
Purple
Filler
Summer

Clematis
Clematis lanuginosa
Purple
Face
Year-round

Veronica
Veronica longifolia
Purple
Gesture
Year-round

China aster
Callistephus chinensis
Double blue
Filler
Summer

Lavender
Lavandula x *intermedia*
Lavender
Gesture / Texture
Year-round

Hydrangea
Hydrangea macrophylla
Pale purple variegated
Filler
Year-round

Hyacinth
Hyacinthus orientalis
'Delft Blue'
Filler
Spring

Forget-me-not
Myosotis sylvatica
Blue
Gesture
Winter / Spring

Larkspur
Consolida regalis
Pale blue
Gesture / Texture
Year-round

Muscari
Muscari botryoides
Blue
Gesture / Texture
Winter / Spring

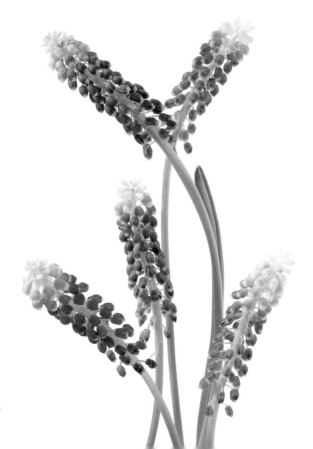

Allium
Allium caeruleum
Blue
Gesture
Spring

Tweedia
Tweedia caerulea
Blue
Filler
Year-round

Cornflower
Centaurea cyanus
Blue
Gesture / Filler
Spring

Iris
Iris latifolia
Blue
Gesture / Filler
Spring

Blue thistle
Eryngium planum
Blue
Texture
Year-round

Delphinium
Delphinium
Blue
Gesture / Face
Year-round

Hydrangea
Hydrangea macrophylla
Blue
Filler
Year-round

Larkspur
Consolida regalis
Dark blue
Gesture / Texture
Year-round

Columbine
Aquilegia vulgaris var.*stellata*
'Black Barlow'
Gesture / Texture
Summer

Bearded iris
Iris germanica
'Black Knight'
Face
Spring

Scabiosa
Scabiosa atropurpurea
Dark red
Gesture
Year-round

Tree peony
Paeonia x *suffruticosa*
'Vesuvian'
Face
Spring

Gerbera daisy
Gerbera x *hybrida*
Dark red
Face / Filler
Year-round

Peony
Paeonia lactiflora
'Black Panther'
Face
Spring

Spray carnation
Dianthus
Pink and purple variegated
Texture / Filler
Year-round

Lady's slipper orchid
Paphiopedilum
Burgundy
Face
Year-round

Tree peony
Paeonia x *suffruticosa*
'Burgundy Wine'
Face
Spring

Plumosa celosia
Celosia argentea
Dark red
Texture / Filler
Summer / Fall

Cosmos
Cosmos bipinnatus
'Rubenza'
Gesture
Summer

Rose
Rosa
'Flash Night'
Filler
Year-round

Parrot tulip
Tulipa
'Rococo'
Gesture
Spring

Martagon hybrid
Lilium x *dalhansonii*
Dark red
Gesture / Texture
Year-round

Zinnia
Zinnia elegans
Persian carpet mix
Texture / Filler
Summer / Fall

Tulip
Tulipa
Brown
Gesture
Spring

Cymbidium orchid
Cymbidium hybrid
Brown
Face / Gesture
Year-round

Fritillaria
Fritillaria uva-vulpis
Brown and yellow
Gesture
Spring

Pitcher plant
Sarracenia x *moorei*
Dark burgundy
Texture
Summer

Calla lily
Zantedeschia
'Red Star'
Gesture / Filler
Year-round

Carnation
Dianthus
Dark purple
Filler
Year-round

Tulip
Tulipa
'Black Jack'
Gesture
Spring

Black Eyed Susan
Rudbeckia hirta
'Cherry Brandy'
Face / Filler
Summer

Sunflower
Helianthus annuus
'Black Beauty'
Face
Summer

Fritillaria
Fritillaria persica
Dark purple
Face / Gesture
Winter / Spring

Dahlia
Dahlia
'Kokucho'
Face
Fall

Dahlia
Dahlia
'Crossfield Ebony'
Face / Filler
Summer / Fall

Dahlia
Dahlia
'Karma Choc'
Face
Summer / Fall

Ranunculus
Ranunculus asiaticus
Black
Face / Filler
Winter / Spring

Cosmos
Cosmos atrosanguineus
'Chocamocha'
Gesture
Summer / Fall

Hellebore
Helleborus x *hybridus*
Double black
Face / Filler
Winter / Spring

412

Anthurium
Anthurium
'Karma Black'
Face
Year-round

Scabiosa
Scabiosa atropurpurea
Black
Gesture
Year-round

Calla lily
Zantedeschia
'Black Star'
Gesture
Year-round

Appendices

Notes

Before You Shop

Know what occasion you are buying for, for example, are you making a large centerpiece for a dinner party, or do you just want to fill a simple vase with a single variety for your home? The questions to ask yourself are: what is the occasion, and where are the flowers going to be placed?

Farmers' markets are great places for buying flowers for your home, as they are often direct from local growers.

Notes

Basic Flower Care

In the end, all flower care comes down to hydration—the better hydrated the flowers, the fresher they'll look and the longer they'll last.

As soon as you get home from the market, anything that's going into water needs a fresh, angled cut.

Always use sharp clippers. Blunt ones can crush the stems and stop them from absorbing water.

Make sure that all buckets used for conditioning, and your vessels for arranging, are scrubbed clean with soap and water. Residue bacteria will cause flowers to die faster.

Add flower food (a sugary mix that you can buy or make yourself) to the water.

Most flowers should go in cold water, but some varieties with harder stems—such as peonies and roses—can be placed into warm or room temperature water to open up faster. This speeds up the absorption of water to the flower head.

Trim or pull off bottom leaves so that there are no leaves below the water line (this can encourage bacteria in the water) and fewer leaves help the flowers hydrate faster.

Always place flowers in a cool place, as heat causes them to wilt. Avoid drafts.

Woody-stemmed flowers, such as lilac, need a bit of work to allow maximum water absorption. Shave off the outer

layer of the lower stem and then cut upwards into the stem multiple times creating a shredded look.

Poppies need to be cauterised before adding to water. To do this, burn the bottom inch or two of the stem with a lighter or other fire source after a fresh cut before placing it in cold water.

Hydrangeas drink from their petals too, so mist the petals as well as putting the stems in water. In fact, most flowers do well with misting, especially if it's hot—and for arrangements done in advance of your events and special occasions, misting them keeps them fresh.

Notes

Essential Tools

Clippers (secateurs):
- for cutting flower stems and greens, keep sharpened so that they don't crush the stems when you cut

Garden shears:
- for cutting branches and woody stems

Floral knife:
- to shave down outer stems or bark, and can also be used to cut stems

Clear floral tape:
- this is more durable than regular clear sticky tapes, used to make tape grids on glass and transparent vessels, for which you couldn't use chicken wire

Green-coated floral wire (this is our magic tool!):
- a very versatile tool used to fasten and secure florals into installations, wreathes, headpieces, and more, it comes in different gauges

Wire clippers (for cutting wire):
- don't use your floral clippers to cut wire as this will quickly blunt them

Floral pin frog (Kenzan):
- for use in glass bowls and shallow vessels to hold stems in place, often used in ikebana

Floral Putty:
–   an adhesive putty used to adhere floral frogs to the
    bottom of vessels as well as other floral elements to
    a large variety of surfaces

Coated chicken wire:
–   used as a base structure for arrangements and
    installations

Green floral sticks:
–   used for spearing fruit to add it to arrangements, as well
    as for lengthening stems by attaching water picks

Green floral tape:
–   a strong floral tape used for most adhesive needs
–   used to attach water picks to floral sticks
–   used for taping chicken wire structures into any vessel
    that is not glass—specifically metal or stone

Water pick:
–   to lengthen flowers that need to be kept in water,
    place stem in water-filled pick and then tape to green
    floral stick
–   to use in installation work when flowers need to be
    in water

Notes

Preparing Vessels

Tapered pitchers and narrow, tall vases:
– good for single-variety bunches of flowers and branches
– no special preparation required; just clean before use

Cylindrical and flared vases:
– great for DIY flower arrangements
– create a simple grid at the top with clear floral tape so that flowers stay in their place.
– to be really precise, pair a floral frog with a tighter tape grid
– the more grid squares you have, the more precise you can be

Glass bowls and compotes:
– adhere a floral frog to the bottom of the bowl with floral putty and combine with a clear tape grid for maximum structure

Footed bowls, urns and compotes:
– this is one of our standard vessels for centerpieces as the foot gives extra height to allow the arrangement to cascade over the rim for movement
– if the vase is opaque, we use chicken wire for structure:
  – cut a square piece of chicken wire 3 ½ times the size of the opening of the vessel
  – connect the four sides of the square to create a box, then bend in the corners to create a ball
  – fit the wire ball into the vase
  – create an 'X' with floral tape over the chicken wire to hold it in place
  – when placing the flowers, make sure the stems go through two layers of chicken wire so they are secure

Notes

Suggested Color Palettes

- White, cream, green and blush
- Chartreuse, light yellow, cream and white
- Peach, light yellow, cream and brown
- Yellow, lavender and white
- Orange, peach and gold with pop of blue
- Rust, coral, red and cream
- Pink, brown and white
- Blue, yellow and cream
- Lavender, chartreuse and dark green
- Mauve, blush and dark burgundy
- Burgundy, deep green and fuchsia
- Purple, cream and black

Notes

Notes on Sustainability

We live in a global society, where flowers are transported everywhere. We realize that the flower industry can be incredibly wasteful at times. Large events, especially, can be a huge source of waste as the flowers are often thrown out straight afterward. However—especially for professional event planners and florists—taking small steps in the right direction can help sustainability:

Shop locally for in-season flowers as much as possible.

Compost all organic matter after events. Include this cost in your budgets.

Share the wealth. In some cities there are now services that will collect flowers for redistribution to hospitals and other institutions.

Avoid single-use materials that are bad for the environment, such as floral foam. Floral frogs, chicken wire and vessels can all be reused.

Notes

Tweedia
Tweedia caerulea
'Pint White'
Filler
Year-round

Hydrangea
Hydrangea macrophylla
White
Filler
Year-round

Cyclamen
Cyclamen persicum
White
Filler
Spring

Azalea
Rhododendron molle
White
Filler
Spring

Ranunculus
Ranunculus asiaticus
Double white
Face / Filler
Winter / Spring

Stock
Matthiola incana
Double white
Gesture / Filler
Year-round

Kangaroo paw
Anigozanthos
'Bush Diamond'
Gesture / Texture
Year-round

Flowering cherry
Prunus x subhirtella
'Autumnalis' white
Gesture / Filler
Spring

Rose
Rosa
'Tibet'
Filler
Year-round

Paper white
Narcissus papyraceus
White
Filler
Winter / spring

Delphinium
Delphinium
'Centurion White'
Face / Gesture
Year-round

Flannel flower
Actinotus helianthi
White
Filler / Texture
Winter / Spring

Scabiosa
Scabiosa columbaria
White
Gesture
Year-round

Spray carnation
Dianthus
'Grenadin White'
Texture / Filler
Year-round

Lily
Lilium
'Premium Blond'
Face
Year-round

Allium / Naples onion
Allium neapolitanum
White
Gesture / Texture
Spring / Summer

Anemone
Anemone
De Caen Group white
Face
Winter / Spring

Spirea
Spiraea
'Arguta'
Gesture / Texture
Winter / Spring

Anemone
Anemone coronaria
Single white
Face
Winter / Spring

Nerine
Nerine bowdenii
'Pallida' white
Filler / Texture
Year-round

Peony
Paeonia
'Bowl of Cream'
Face
Spring

Spray carnation
Dianthus
'Star Snow
  Tessino'
Filler / Texture
Year-round

Rose
Rosa
'White Majolica'
Filler
Year-round

Rose
Rosa
Winchester
  Cathedral 'Auscat'
Face / Filler
Spring / Fall

Lilac
Syringa vulgaris
White
Filler
Spring

Astrantia
Astrantia major
'White Giant'
Texture / Filler
Year-round

Calla lily
*Zantedeschia
  aethiopica*
White
Face / Gesture
Year-round

Amaryllis
Hippeastrum
'White Dazzler'
Face
Winter

Freesia
Freesia
White
Filler
Year-round

Gladiolus
Gladiolus
'White Prosperity'
Gesture
Year-round

Gladiolus
Gladiolus x
  colvillii
'Albus'
Gesture
Summer / Fall

Dahlia
Dahlia
'Blizzard'
Face
Summer / Fall

Rose
Rosa
'Garden Snow'
Filler
Year-round

Hyacinth
*Hyacinthus
  orientalis*
White
Filler
Winter / Spring

Tulip
Tulipa
'White Liberstar'
Gesture
Spring

Narcissus
*Narcissus
  poeticus* hybrid
White
Face / Filler
Winter / Spring

Gooseneck
  loosestrife
*Lysimachia
  clethroides*
White
Gesture
Summer

Muscari
Muscari azureum
'Album'
Texture / Filler
Winter / Spring

Solomon's seal
*Polygonatum
  biflorum*
White
Gesture
Spring

Lily of
  the valley
*Convallaria
  majalis*
White
Texture
Spring

Snowflake / *Leucojum aestivum* / White / Texture / Winter	**Sweet pea** / *Lathyrus odoratus* / White / Texture / Filler / Gesture / Winter / Spring	**Gerbera daisy** / *Gerbera x hybrida* / White / Face / Gesture / Year-round	**Lisianthus** / *Eustoma russellianum* / White / Filler / Year-round
Tulip / *Tulipa* / 'Honeymoon' / Gesture / Spring	**Gladiolus** / *Gladiolus* / 'The Bride' / Gesture / Filler / Summer	**Astilbe** / *Astilbe* / 'Deutschland' / Texture / Year-round	**Everlasting pea** / *Lathyrus latifolius* / 'Albus' white / Texture / Filler / Gesture / Winter / Spring
Cosmos / *Cosmos bipinnatus* / Double white / Gesture / Summer	**Dahlia** / *Dahlia* / 'Figaro' White / Face / Summer / Fall	**Anthurium** / *Anthurium* / 'Acropolis' / Face / Year-round	**Calla lily** / *Zantedeschia* / 'Aspen' / Gesture / Year-round
Anthurium / *Anthurium* / 'Lumina' / Face / Year-round	**Peony** / *Paeonia lactiflora* / 'Festiva Maxima' / Face / Spring	**Blue lace flower** / *Trachymene coerulea* / 'Lacy Pink' / Gesture / Spring / Summer	**Nigella** / *Nigella damascena* / White / Texture / Spring / Summer
Spirea / *Spiraea thunbergii* / White / Gesture / Texture / Winter / Spring	**Heath rice flower** / *Pimelea phylicoides* / White / Texture / Spring / Summer	**Wax flower** / *Chamelaucium uncinatum* / White / Texture / Filler / Year-round	**Quince** / *Chaenomeles speciosa* / 'Nivalis' white / Gesture / Winter

Peony
*Paeonia
  lactiflora*
'Duchesse
  de Nemours'
Face
Spring

Sweet pea
*Lathyrus
  odoratus*
Pale pink
Texture / Filler /
  Gesture
Winter / Spring

Peony
*Paeonia
  lactiflora*
'Rooster Reveille'
Face
Spring

Peony
*Paeonia
  lactiflora*
'Sonata'
Face
Spring

Foxglove
*Digitalis
  purpurea*
f. albiflora
Gesture / Face
Spring / Summer

Dogwood
Cornus kousa
var. *chinensis*
Gesture / Filler
Spring

Oncidium orchid
Oncidium hybrid
White and pink
Texture / Gesture
Year-round

Butterfly
  ranunculus
*Ranunculus
  asiaticus*
'Butterfly Lux'
  cream
Gesture / Filler
Winter / Spring

Narcissus
Narcissus
'Salome'
Face / Filler
Spring

Jasmine
*Jasminum
  polyanthum*
White and pink
Texture
Winter / Spring

Rose
Rosa
'Charity'
Filler
Spring / Fall

Rose
Rosa
'Champagne'
Filler
Year-round

Hyacinth
*Hyacinthus
  orientalis*
Pale pink
Filler
Winter / Spring

Astilbe
Astilbe
'Elizabeth Bloom'
Texture
Year-round

Stock
Matthiola incana
Double peach
Filler /
  Gesture
Year-round

Lily
Lilium
Pink roselily
Face
Year-round

Rose
Rosa
'Sahara'
Filler
Year-round

Epidendrum
Epidendrum
  hybrid
Pale pink
Gesture
Year-round

Chrysanthemum
Chrysanthemum
'Seaton's Je Dore'
Face
Fall

Dahlia
Dahlia
'Cream and
  Pink'
Face
Summer / Fall

Pansy
Viola hybrid
Pale pink and
  yellow
Filler
Winter / Spring
	Statice
	Limonium
	  sinuatum
	Peach
	Texture
	Year-round
		Bearded iris
		Iris germanica
		'Party Dress'
		Face
		Spring
			Tulip
			Tulipa
			'Apricot Beauty'
			Gesture
			Spring

Carnation *Dianthus* Nude Filler Year-round	Rose *Rosa* 'Sahara Sensation' Filler Year-round	Stock *Matthiola incana* Single petal peach Gesture / Filler Year-round	Rose *Rosa* 'Cappuccino' Filler Year-round
Lily *Lilium* Peach Face Year-round	Lisianthus *Eustoma* *russellianum* Peach Filler Year-round	Rose *Rosa* Juliet 'Ausjameson' Face / Filler Year-round	Dahlia *Dahlia* 'Cafe au Lait' Face Summer / Fall
Tree peony *Paeonia* x *suffruticosa* 'Kopper Kettle' Face Spring	Dogwood *Cornus kousa* Pink Gesture / Filler Spring	Rose *Rosa* 'Pink Majolica' Filler Year-round	Rose *Rosa* 'Emily' Filler Year-round
Rose *Rosa* 'Tango' Face / Filler Spring / Fall	Ranunculus *Ranunculua* *asiaticus* Double peach Face / Filler Winter / Spring	Gerbera daisy *Gerbera* x *hybrida* Apricot Face / Gesture Year-round	Rose *Rosa* 'Distant Drum' Face / Filler Sping / Fall

Calla lily
Zantedeschia
'Kiwi Blush'
Gesture
Year-round

Rose
Rosa
'Quicksand'
Filler
Year-round

Parrot tulip
Tulipa
'Libretto Parrot'
Gesture
Spring

Phalaenopsis
orchid
*Phalaenopsis
hybrid*
Pale yellow and
pink
Face / Filler /
Gesture
Year-round

Peony
*Paeonia
lactiflora*
'Lady Gay'
Face
Spring

Rose
Rosa
'Secret Garden'
Filler
Year-round

Foxglove
*Digitalis
purpurea*
Pale pink
Gesture / Face
Spring / Summer

Ranunculus
*Ranunculus
asiaticus*
Double pink
Face / Filler
Winter / Spring

Coxcomb
Celosia cristata
Green and pale
pink
Filler
Summer / Fall

Rose
Rosa
'Caffe Latte'
Face / Filler
Year-round

Carnation
Dianthus
Variegated
Filler
Year-round

Rose
Rosa
'Pink Raddish'
Texture / Filler
Year-round

Lilac
Syringa vulgaris
'Beauty of Moscow'
Filler
Spring

Yarrow
*Achillea
millefolium*
Pink-purple
Filler / Texture
Year-round

Celosia
Celosia spicata
Pink-purple
Gesture / Texture
Summer / Fall

Rose
Rosa
'Amnesia'
Filler
Year-round

Sweet pea
*Lathyrus
odoratus*
Lavender
Texture / Filler /
Gesture
Winter / Spring

Larkspur
*Consolida
regalis*
Pale pink
Filler / Texture
Year-round

Cherry blossom
*Prunus
glandulosa*
'Sinensis' double
pink
Gesture / Filler
Spring

Tuberose
*Polianthes
tuberosa*
'Pink Sapphire'
Gesture
Year-round

449

Agapanthus
Agapanthus
 praecox
Blue
Texture / Filler
Year-round

Statice
Limonium
 sinuatum
Pale blue
Filler
Year-round

Scabiosa
Scabiosa
 caucasica
Pale blue
Gesture
Year-round

Campanula /
 bellflower
Campanula
 medium
Pale blue
Filler
Spring / Summer

Fritilaria
Fritillaria
 hermonis
Green and brown
Gesture
Spring

Allium
Allium cepa
'Snake Ball'
Gesture
Spring

Blue star
Amsonia
 tabernaemontana
Blue
Texture / Filler
Summer

Nigella
Nigella
 damascena
Blue
Texture
Spring/ Summer

Fritillaria
Fritillaria
 persica
'Ivory Bells'
Face / Gesture
Spring

Hellebore
Helleborus x
 hybridus
Double green
 and purple
Face / Filler
Winter / Spring

Fritillaria
Fritillaria
 pontica
Green and brown
Gesture
Spring

Coxcomb
Celosia cristata
Pale green
Filler
Summer / Fall

Vibernum
Viburnum opulus
'Roseum'
Filler
Spring

Tulip
Tulipa
'White Parrot'
Gesture
Spring

Tuberose
Polianthes
 tuberosa
'The Pearl'
Gesture
Year-round

Hellebore
Helleborus x
 hybridus
Green and cream
Face / Filler
Winter / Spring

Allium /
 Sicilian onion
Allium siculum
Cream and brown
Texture
Spring

Hellebore
Helleborus x
 hybridus
Green and purple
Face / Filler
Winter / Spring

French parrot
 tulip
Tulipa
Green
Gesture
Spring

Ranunculus
Ranunculus
 asiaticus
Double green
Face / Filler
Winter / Spring

Hydrangea
Hydrangea
macrophylla
Brown and
pink
Filler
Year-round

Hellebore /
Christmas rose
Helleborus niger
Brown
Face / Filler
Winter / Spring

Queen Anne's
lace
Daucus carota
'Dara'
Gesture / Texture
Summer / Fall

Andromeda
Pieris japonica
White
Texture / Filler
Winter / Spring

Kangaroo paw
Anigozanthos
Pink and orange
Texture
Year-round

Wax flower
Chamelaucium
uncinatum
Pink and white
variegated
Texture / Filler
Year-round

Rose
Rosa
'Koko Loko'
Face / Filler
Spring / Fall

Foxtail lily
Eremurus
robustus
Peach
Gesture
Spring / Summer

Rose
Rosa
'Golden Mustard'
Filler
Year-round

Grevillea
Grevillea
pteridifolia
Pale yellow
Gesture / Texture
Year-round

Snake's head
fritillary
Fritillaria
meleagris
Purple
Gesture /
Texture
Spring

Ranunculus
Ranunculus
asiaticus
Double white and
brown
Face / Filler
Winter / Spring

Easter lily
Lilium
longiflorum
White
Face
Year-round

Narcissus
Narcissus
'Bridal Crown'
Filler
Winter / Spring

Chamomile
Matricaria
chamomilla
White and yellow
Texture / Filler
Year-round

Scabiosa
Scabiosa
atropurpurea
Pale cream
Gesture
Year-round

Rose
Rosa
Crocus Rose
'Ausquest'
Face / Filler
Spring / Fall

Lady's slipper
orchid
Paphiopedilum
Yellow
Face
Year-round

Daisy mum
Chrysanthemum
Hybrid yellow
Filler
Year-round

Peony
Paeonia
lactiflora
'Day Star'
Face
Spring

Gloriosa lily *Gloriosa* *superba* 'Lutea' Texture / Gesture Year-round	**Narcissus** *Narcissus* 'Tahiti' Gesture / Filler Spring	**Peony** *Paeonia* *lactiflora* 'Lemon Dream' Face Spring	**Peony** *Paeonia* *lactiflora* 'Claire de Lune' Face Spring
Freesia *Freesia* Double yellow Filler Year-round	**Tulip** *Tulipa* 'Yellow Flight' Gesture Spring	**Pansy** *Viola* hybrid Yellow Filler Winter / spring	**Forsythia** *Forsythia x* *intermedia* Yellow Gesture / Texture Spring
French parrot tulip *Tulipa* Yellow Gesture Spring	**Butterfly ranunculus** *Ranunculus* *asiaticus* Yellow Gesture / Filler Winter / Spring	**Gerbera daisy** *Gerbera* x *hybrida* Butter yellow Face Year-round	**Tulip** *Tulipa* 'Monte Spider' Gesture Spring
Mimosa *Acacia* *retinodes* Yellow Filler / Texture Winter / Spring	**Goldenrod** *Solidago* *canadensis* Yellow Filler / Texture Summer / Fall	**Oncidium orchid** *Oncidium* Hybrid yellow Filler / Gesture Year-round	**Witch hazel** *Hamamelis x* *intermedia* Yellow Gesture / Texture Winter / Spring
Calendula *Calendula* *officinalis* Yellow Filler Spring / Summer	**Yarrow** *Achillea* *filipendulina* Gold Filler / Texture Year-round	**Daffodil** *Narcissus* *pseudonarcissus* Yellow Face Winter / Spring	**Narcissus** *Narcissus* 'Soleil d'Or' Filler Winter / Spring

French tulip
Tulipa
Yellow and red
Gesture
Spring

French marigold
Tagetes patula
Striped mix
Texture / Gesture
Summer

Sunflower
*Helianthus
   annuus*
Yellow
Face
Summer

Ranunculus
*Ranunculus
   asiaticus*
Clooney series,
   double yellow
Face / Filler
Winter / Spring

Lady's slipper
   orchid
*Paphiopedilum
   hybrid*
Brown and green
Face
Year-round

Sweet pea
*Lathyrus
   odoratus*
Yellow dyed
Texture / Filler /
   Gesture
Winter / Spring

Coxcomb
Celosia cristata
Yellow
Filler
Summer / Fall

Oncidium orchid
Oncidium
Yellow
Gesture / Texture
Year-round

Golden lantern
   lily
*Sandersonia
   aurantiaca*
Orange
Gesture / Texture
Spring / Summer

Butterfly
   ranunculus
*Ranunculus
   asiaticus*
Single orange
Gesture / Filler
Winter / Spring

Rose
Rosa
'Combo'
Filler
Year-round

Lily
Lilium
'Solange'
Face
Year-round

Gloriosa lily
Gloriosa superba
Orange
Gesture
Year-round

Butterfly weed
*Asclepias
   tuberosa*
Orange
Filler /
   Texture
Year-round

Dahlia
Dahlia
'Lakeview Lucky'
Face / Filler
Summer / Fall

Calendula
*Calendula
   officinalis*
'Indian Prince'
Filler
Spring / Summer

Pincushion protea
Leucospermum
'Carnival Orange'
Face / Texture
Year-round

Ranunculus
*Ranunculus
   asiaticus*
Gold and red
   variegated
Face / Filler
Winter / Spring

Birds of
   paradise
*Strelitzia
   reginae*
Orange
Face / Gesture
Year-round

Narcissus
Narcissus
'Johann Strauss'
Filler
Spring

Fritillaria
Fritillaria
 imperialis
Orange
Face / Gesture
Spring

Orange
 chincherinchee
Ornithogalum
 dubium
Orange
Filler
Year-round

Ranunculus
Ranunculus
 asiaticus
Double orange
Face / Filler
Winter / Spring

Epidendrum
Epidendrum
 hybrid
Orange
Face / Gesture
Year-round

Gomphrena
Gomphrena
 globosa
Orange
Filler
Summer / Fall

Ranunculus
Ranunculus
 asiaticus
Clooney series,
 peach
Face / Filler
Winter / Spring

Rose
Rosa
Renaissance
 series 'Claire'
Face / Filler
Spring / Fall

Icelandic poppy
Papaver nudicaule
Peach
Face / Gesture
Winter / Spring

French tulip
Tulipa
'Flaming Parrot'
Gesture
Spring

Martagon hybrid
Lilium x *martagon*
'Orange Marmalade'
Gesture / Texture
Summer

Calla lily
Zantedeschia
'Mango'
Gesture / Filler
Year-round

Anthurium
Anthurium
'Rothschildianum'
Face
Year-round

Plumosa celosia
Celosia argentea
Rust
Filler / Texture
Summer / Fall

Heliconia
Heliconia
 stricta
Red
Face
Year-round

Icelandic poppy
Papaver nudicaule
Orange
Gesture / Face
Winter / Spring

Dahlia
Dahlia
'Iced Tea'
Face / Filler
Summer / Fall

Anthurium
Anthurium
'Hawaii'
Face
Year-round

Rose
Rosa
'Toffee'
Filler
Year-round

Spider mum
Chrysanthemum
Orange and
 yellow
Face / Filler
Fall

Tulip
Tulipa
'Leo'
Gesture
Spring

James Story
  orchid
Oncidium hybrid
Yellow and brown
Gesture / Texture
Year-round

Oncidium orchid
Oncidium hybrid
Orange and
  brown
Gesture / Texture
Year-round

Spider mum
Chrysanthemum
'Seaton's Toffee'
Face / Filler
Fall

Coxcomb
Celosia cristata
Rust
Filler
Summer / Fall

Ranunculus
Ranunculus
  asiaticus
'Charlotte' peach
Face
Winter / Spring

Sweet pea
Lathyrus
  odoratus
Brown dyed
Texture / Filler /
  Gesture
Winter / Spring

Pitcher plant
Sarracenia
  leucophylla
Red and white
  variegated
Texture
Spring / Summer

Amaryllis
Hippeastrum
  cybister
'Tarantula'
Face
Winter

Dahlia
Dahlia
'Gitts Crazy'
Face
Summer / Fall

Dahlia
Dahlia
'Cornel Bronze'
Face / Filler
Summer / Fall

Dahlia
Dahlia
'Bahama Apricot'
Face
Summer / Fall

Beared iris
Iris germanica
Purple and brown
Face
Spring

Amaryllis
Hippeastrum
'Rilona'
Face
Winter

Rose
Rosa
'Kahala'
Filler
Year-round

Tree peony
Paeonia x
  suffruticosa
'Callie's Memory'
Face
Spring

Anthurium
Anthurium
'Cognac'
Face
Year-round

Icelandic poppy
Papaver
  nudicaule
Watermelon
Face / Gesture
Winter / Spring

Quince
Chaenomeles
  japonica
Coral
Gesture
Winter / Spring

Zinnia
Zinnia elegans
Coral
Face / Filler
Summer

Quince
Chaenomeles
  speciosa
Red
Gesture
Winter / Spring

Carnation
Dianthus
Pink and red
Filler
Year-round

Dahlia
Dahlia
Pale red
Face / Filler
Summer / Fall

Christmas bush
Ceratopetalum
gummiferum
'Albery's Red'
Texture / Filler
Fall / Winter

Dahlia
Dahlia
'Amber Queen'
Face / Filler
Summer / Fall

French tulip
Tulipa
'Kingsblood'
Gesture
Spring

Dahlia
Dahlia
'Red and White
Fubuki'
Face
Summer / Fall

Butterfly
ranunculus
Ranunculus
asiaticus
Double rust
Gesture / Filler
Winter / Spring

Cosmos
Cosmos
atrosanguineus
Dark red
Gesture
Summer / Fall

Gerbera daisy
Gerbera x
hybrida
Red
Face
Year-round

Quill
Tillandsia
cyanea hybrid
Red
Filler
Year-round

Amaryllis
Hippeastrum
'Simply Red'
Face
Winter

Heliconia
Heliconia
vellerigera
'King Kong'
Face
Year-round

Spray carnation
Dianthus
'Solomio Amos'
Texture / Filler
Year-round

French parrot
tulip
Tulipa
'Red Parrot'
Gesture
Spring

Cyclamen
Cyclamen
persicum
Red
Filler
Spring

Anthurium
Anthurium
andraeanum
Red
Face
Year-round

Coxcomb
Celosia cristata
Dark red
Filler
Summer / Fall

Ranunculus
Ranunculus
asiaticus
Dark red
Face / Filler
Winter / Spring

Anemone
Anemone
coronaria
Red
Face
Winter / Spring

Zinnia
Zinnia elegans
Double red
Face / Filler
Summer

Tulip
Tulipa
'Black Hero'
Gesture
Spring

Rose
Rosa
Black Magic
'Tankalcig'
Filler
Year-round

Dahlia
Dahlia
Dark red
Face
Summer / Fall

Rose
Rosa
'Red Piano'
Face / Filler
Year-round

Straw flower
Xerochrysum
 bracteatum
Burgundy
Filler / Texture
Summer / Fall

Peony
Paeonia
 lactiflora
'Chocolate Soldier'
Face
Spring

Peony
Paeonia
 lactiflora
'Black Swan'
Face
Spring

Ranunculus
Ranunculus
 asiaticus
Red and brown
 variegated
Face / Filler
Winter / Spring

Lisianthus
Eustoma
 russellianum
Brown and purple
 variegated
Filler
Year-round

Cymbidium orchid
Cymbidium hybrid
Dark pink
Face / Gesture
Year-round

Hydrangea
Hydrangea
 macrophylla
Dark pink
Filler
Year-round

Astilbe
Astilbe
'Red Sentinel'
Texture
Year-round

Dahlia
Dahlia
'Sonic Bloom'
Face
Summer / Fall

Anenome
Anemone
 coronaria
Red and white
 variegated
Face
Winter / Spring

Ranunculus
Ranunculus
 asiaticus
Dark pink
Face / Filler
Winter / Spring

Tree peony
Paeonia x
 suffruticosa
Dark pink and peach
Face
Spring

Rose
Rosa
'Pink Piano'
Face / Filler
Year-round

Azalea
Rhododendron
 molle
Pink hybrid
Filler
Spring

Sweet pea
Lathyrus
 odoratus
Red
Texture / Filler /
 Gesture
Winter / Spring

Ginger
Alpinia
 purpurata
Red
Face
Year-round

Ranunculus *Ranunculus asiaticus* Double pink and green Face / Filler Winter / Spring	Sweet pea *Lathyrus odoratus* Coral Texture / Filler / Gesture Winter / Spring	Rose *Rosa* 'Pink Floyd' Filler Year-round	Rose *Rosa* Kate 'Auschris' Face / Filler Spring / Fall
Rose *Rosa* 'Romantic Antike' Face / Filler Year-round	Waratah *Telopea speciosissima* Pink Face / Texture Summer / Fall	Rose *Rosa* Benjamin Britten 'Ausencart' Face / Filler Spring / Fall	Peony *Paeonia* 'Coral Charm' Face Spring
Ranunculus *Ranunculus asiaticus* Double pink Face / Filler Winter / Spring	Rose *Rosa* 'Lady Moon' Filler Year-round	Peony *Paeonia lactiflora* 'Dr Alexander Fleming' Face Spring	Anthurium *Anthurium* 'Marea' Face Year-round
Bleeding heart *Lamprocapnos spectabilis* Pink Gesture / Texture Spring	Statice *Limonium sinuatum* Pink Filler Year-round	Lisianthus *Eustoma russellianum* Double pink Filler Year-round	French tulip *Tulipa* Pink Gesture Spring
Water lily *Nymphaea* Pink Face Year-round	Ranunculus *Ranunculus asiaticus* 'Charlotte' burgundy and white Face Winter / Spring	Peony *Paeonia lactiflora* 'Nymphe' Face Spring	Dahlia *Dahlia* 'Lagoon' Face Summer / Fall

Ranunculus
Ranunculus asiaticus
Clooney series, pale pink
Face / Filler
Winter / Spring

Peony
Paeonia lactiflora
'Sarah Bernhardt'
Face
Spring

Scabiosa
Scabiosa columbaria
Pink
Gesture
Year-round

Echinacea
Echinacea purpurea
Pink
Face / Filler
Summer

Anemone
Anemone coronaria
Double magenta
Face
Winter / Spring

Rose
Rosa
'Royal Amethyst'
Face / Filler
Spring / Fall

Magnolia
Magnolia x *soulangeana*
'Alexandrina'
Face / Gesture
Spring

Plum blossom
Prunus mume
Pink
Gesture
Spring

Hellebore
Helleborus x *hybridus*
Dark pink
Face / Filler
Winter

Gerbera daisy
Gerbera x *hybrida*
Double dark pink
Face
Year-round

Autumn anemone / Japanese anemone
Anemone hupehensis
Pale purple
Gesture
Fall

Sedum
Hylotelephium telephium
Pink
Filler
Summer / Fall

Sweet pea
Lathyrus odoratus
Purple and white variegated
Texture / Filler / Gesture
Winter / Spring

Foxglove
Digitalis purpurea
Purple
Gesture / Face
Spring / Summer

Grevillea
Grevillea
'Robyn Gordon'
Gesture / Texture
Year-round

Zinnia
Zinnia elegans
'Queen Lime Blush'
Filler
Summer

Sweet William catchfly
Silene armeria
Purple
Texture / Filler
Spring

Boronia
Boronia heterophylla
Purple
Filler / Texture
Spring

Dahlia
Dahlia
'Koko Puff'
Face / Filler
Summer / Fall

Heather
Calluna vulgaris
Dark pink
Texture / Filler
Year-round

Rose
Rosa
'Menta'
Filler
Year-round

Chrysanthemum
Chrysanthemum
Lilac
Filler
Year-round

Dahlia
Dahlia
'Mikayla Miranda'
Face
Summer / Fall

Anthurium
Anthurium
'Previa'
Face
Year-round

Liatris
Liatris spicata
Purple
Gesture
Year-round

Delphinium
Delphinium
Lavender
Gesture / Face
Year-round

Parrot tulip
Tulipa
'Blue Parrot'
Gesture
Spring

Sweet pea
*Lathyrus
  odoratus*
'Matucana'
Texture / Filler /
  Gesture
Winter / Spring

Sweet pea
*Lathyrus
  odoratus*
Chocolate dyed
Texture / Filler /
  Gesture
Winter / Spring

Bearded iris
Iris germanica
'Indian Chief'
Face
Spring

Astrantia
Astrantia major
'Rosensinfonie'
Texture / Filler
Year-round

Ranunculus
*Ranunculus
  asiaticus*
Purple and mauve
  variegated
Face / Filler
Winter / Spring

Lilac
Syringa
Lavender
Texture / Filler
Spring

Allium
Allium cepa
Purple and gray
Gesture
Spring

Hellebore
*Helleborus x
  hybridus*
Dark purple
Face / Filler
Winter / Spring

Lisianthus
*Eustoma
  russellianum*
Dark purple
Filler
Year-round

Clematis
Clematis alpina
'Tage Lundell'
  lavender
Gesture / Filler
Year-round

Lupine
*Lupinus x
  regalis*
Blue
Gesture
Spring / Summer

Sweet pea
*Lathyrus
  odoratus*
'Chocolate Flake'
Texture / Filler /
  Gesture
Winter / Spring

Oncidium orchid
Oncidium hybrid
'Kauai'
Gesture
Year-round

Sweet pea
Lathyrus
 nervosus
Purple
Texture / Filler /
 Gesture
Winter / Spring

Kangaroo paw
Anigozanthos
 flavidus
'Ember' purple
 variegated
Gesture / Texture
Year-round

Bell clematis
Clematis
'Rooguchi' purple
Gesture
Spring

Hellebore
Helleborus x
 hybridus
Double pink and
 white variegated
Face / Filler
Winter / Spring

Anemone
Anemone
 coronaria
Lavender
Face
Winter / Spring

Water lily
Nymphaea
 nouchali
Lavender
Face
Year-round

Cineraria
Pericallis x
 hybrida
Blue
Texture / Filler
Spring

Bell clematis
Clematis
'Rooguchi' blue
Gesture
Spring

China aster
Callistephus
 chinensis
Double blue
Filler
Summer

Veronica
Veronica
 longifolia
Purple
Gesture
Year-round

Clematis
Clematis
 lanuginosa
Purple
Face
Year-round

Floss flower
Ageratum
 houstonianum
Purple
Filler
Summer

Forget-me-not
Myosotis
 sylvatica
Blue
Gesture
Winter / Spring

Hyacinth
Hyacinthus
 orientalis
'Delft Blue'
Filler
Spring

Hydrangea
Hydrangea
 macrophylla
Pale purple
 variegated
Filler
Year-round

Lavender
Lavandula x
 intermedia
Lavender
Gesture / Texture
Year-round

Tweedia
Tweedia caerulea
Blue
Filler
Year-round

Allium
Allium caeruleum
Blue
Gesture
Spring

Muscari
Muscari botryoides
Blue
Gesture / Texture
Winter / Spring

Larkspur
Consolida regalis
Pale blue
Gesture / Texture
Year-round

Delphinium
Delphinium
Blue
Gesture / Face
Year-round

Blue thistle
Eryngium planum
Blue
Texture
Year-round

Iris
Iris latifolia
Blue
Gesture / Filler
Spring

Cornflower
Centaurea cyanus
Blue
Gesture / Filler
Spring

Bearded iris
Iris germanica
'Black Knight'
Face
Spring

Columbine
*Aquilegia
 vulgaris* var.
 stellata
'Black Barlow'
Gesture / Texture
Summer

Larkspur
Consolida regalis
Dark blue
Gesture / Texture
Year-round

Hydrangea
*Hydrangea
 macrophylla*
Blue
Filler
Year-round

Peony
Paeonia lactiflora
'Black Panther'
Face
Spring

Gerbera daisy
*Gerbera x
 hybrida*
Dark red
Face / Filler
Year-round

Tree peony
*Paeonia x
 suffruticosa*
'Vesuvian'
Face
Spring

Scabiosa
*Scabiosa
 atropurpurea*
Dark red
Gesture
Year-round

Plumosa celosia
Celosia argentea
Dark red
Texture / Filler
Summer / Fall

Tree peony
*Paeonia x
 suffruticosa*
'Burgundy Wine'
Face
Spring

Lady's slipper
orchid
Paphiopedilum
Burgundy
Face
Year-round

Spray carnation
Dianthus
Pink and purple
variegated
Texture / Filler
Year-round

Martagon hybrid
Lilium x dalhansonii
Dark red
Gesture / Texture
Year-round

Parrot tulip
Tulipa
'Rococo'
Gesture
Spring

Rose
Rosa
'Flash Night'
Filler
Year-round

Cosmos
Cosmos bipinnatus
'Rubenza'
Gesture
Summer

Fritillaria
Fritillaria uva-vulpis
Brown and yellow
Gesture
Spring

Cymbidium orchid
Cymbidium hybrid
Brown
Face / Gesture
Year-round

Tulip
Tulipa
Brown
Gesture
Spring

Zinnia
Zinnia elegans
Persian carpet mix
Texture / Filler
Summer / Fall

Tulip
Tulipa
'Black Jack'
Gesture
Spring

Carnation
Dianthus
Dark purple
Filler
Year-round

Calla lily
Zantedeschia
'Red Star'
Gesture / Filler
Year-round

Pitcher plant
Sarracenia x *moorei*
Dark burgundy
Texture
Summer

Dahlia
Dahlia
'Kokucho'
Face
Fall

Fritillaria
Fritillaria persica
Dark purple
Face / Gesture
Winter / Spring

Sunflower
Helianthus annuus
'Black Beauty'
Face
Summer

Black eyed Susan
Rudbeckia hirta
'Cherry Brandy'
Face / Filler
Summer

Cosmos
Cosmos atrosanguineus
'Chocamocha'
Gesture
Summer / Fall

Ranunculus
Ranunculus asiaticus
Black
Face / Filler
Winter / Spring

Dahlia
Dahlia
'Karma Choc'
Face
Summer / Fall

Dahlia
Dahlia
'Crossfield Ebony'
Face / Filler
Summer / Fall

Calla lily
Zantedeschia
'Black Star'
Gesture
Year-round

Scabiosa
Scabiosa atropurpurea
Black
Gesture
Year-round

Anthurium
Anthurium
'Karma Black'
Face
Year-round

Hellebore
Helleborus x *hybridus*
Double black
Face / Filler
Winter / Spring

Index of botanical names

A

Acacia retinodes, 191, 453
Achillea filipendulina, 194, 453
Achillea millefolium, 130, 447
Actinotus helianthi, 24, 437
Agapanthus praecox, 139, 449
Ageratum houstonianum, 364, 471
Allium caeruleum, 374, 471
Allium cepa, 350, 469
    'Snake Ball', 142, 449
Allium neapolitanum, 28, 437
Allium siculum, 155, 449
Alpinia purpurata, 292, 463
Amsonia tabernaemontana, 141, 449
Anemone
    Anemone coronaria 33, 273, 290, 323, 363, 437, 461, 463, 467, 471
    De Caen Group white, 35, 437
    Anemone hupehensis, 325, 467
Anigozanthos, 163, 451
    'Bush Diamond', 21, 437
    'Ember', 358, 471
Anthurium
    'Acropolis', 65, 441
    'Cognac', 248, 459
    'Hawaii', 235, 457
    'Karma Black', 413, 475
    'Lumina', 71, 441
    'Marea', 304, 465
    'Previa', 336, 469
    'Rothschildianum', 224, 457
    Anthurium andraeanum, 268, 461
Aquilegia vulgaris var. *stellata*
    'Black Barlow', 382, 473
Asclepias tuberosa, 210, 455
Astilbe
    'Deutschland', 61, 441
    'Elizabeth Bloom'', 90, 443
    'Red Sentinel', 284, 463
Astrantia major
    'Rosensinfonie', 345, 469
    'White Giant', 42, 439

B

Boronia heterophylla, 334, 467

C

Calendula officinalis 195, 453
    'Indian Prince', 208, 455
Callistephus chinensis, 367, 471

Calluna vulgaris, 332, 467
Campanula medium, 136, 449
Celosia argentea, 231, 391, 457, 473
Celosia cristata, 127, 144, 201, 236, 275, 447, 449, 455, 459, 461
Celosia spicata, 129, 447
Centaurea cyanus, 376, 473
Ceratopetalum gummiferum
    'Albery's Red', 257, 461
Chaenomeles japonica, 254, 459
Chaenomeles speciosa, 252, 459
    'Nivalis', 72, 441
Chamelaucium uncinatum, 73, 162, 441, 451
Chrysanthemum, 173, 233, 338, 451, 457, 469
    'Seaton's Je Dore', 93, 443
    'Seaton's Toffee', 237, 459
Clematis
    'Rooguchi', 357, 360, 471
    Clematis alpina 'Tage Lundell', 355, 469
    Clematis lanuginosa, 365, 471
Consolida regalis, 134, 372, 381, 447, 471, 473
Convallaria majalis, 52, 439
Cornus kousa, 110, 445
    var. *chinensis*, 82, 443
Cosmos atrosanguineus, 260, 461
    'Chocamocha', 411, 475
Cosmos bipinnatus, 67, 441
    'Rubenza', 392, 473
Cyclamen persicum 17, 269, 437, 461
Cymbidium hybrid, 286, 398, 463, 475

D

Dahlia, 44, 92, 209, 228, 247, 256, 258, 277, 291, 312, 333, 337, 439, 443, 455, 457, 459, 461, 463, 465, 467, 469
    'Amber Queen', 256, 461
    'Bahama Apricot', 245, 459
    'Cafe au Lait', 104, 445
    'Cornel Bronze', 246, 459
    'Cream and Pink', 92, 443
    'Crossfield Ebony', 408, 475
    'Figaro', 66, 441
    'Gitts Crazy', 247, 459
    'Iced Tea', 228, 457
    'Karma Choc', 409, 475
    'Koko Puff', 333, 467
    'Kokucho', 407, 475
    'Lagoon', 312, 465

'Lakeview Lucky', 209, 455
'Mikayla Miranda', 337, 469
'Red and White Fubuki', 262, 461
'Sonic Bloom', 291, 463
Daucus carota 'Dara', 157, 451
Delphinium, 342, 379, 469, 473
'Centurion White', 25, 437
Dianthus, 103, 125, 259, 388, 402, 445, 447, 461, 473, 475
'Grenadin White', 30, 437
'Solomio Amos', 271, 461
'Star Snow Tessino', 38, 439
Digitalis purpurea, 121, 330, 447, 467
f. albiflora, 83, 443

E

Echinacea purpurea, 316, 467
Epidendrum hybrid, 94, 216, 443, 457
Eremurus robustus, 160, 451
Eryngium planum, 378, 473
Eustoma russellianum, 56, 106, 287, 309, 348, 441, 445, 463, 465, 469

F

Forsythia x intermedia, 180, 453
Freesia, 47, 183, 439, 453
Fritillaria hermonis, 143, 449
Fritillaria imperialis, 219, 457
Fritillaria meleagris, 165, 451
Fritillaria persica, 406, 475
'Ivory Bells', 147, 449
Fritillaria pontica, 145, 449
Fritillaria uva-vulpis, 399, 475

G

Gerbera x hybrida, 57, 113, 185, 267, 326, 386, 441, 445, 453, 461, 467, 473
Gladiolus
'The Bride', 62, 441
'White Prosperity', 46, 439
Gladiolus x convillii 'Albus', 45, 439
Gloriosa superba, 211, 455
'Lutea', 179, 453
Gomphrena globosa, 223, 457
Grevillea
'Robyn Gordon', 329, 467
Grevillea pteridifolia, 166, 451

H

Hamamelis x intermedia, 188, 453
Helianthus annuus, 197, 455
'Black Beauty', 405, 475

Heliconia stricta, 230, 457
Heliconia vellerigera 'King Kong', 264, 461
Helleborus niger, 158, 451
Helleborus x hybridus, 146, 148, 154, 327, 349, 356, 412, 449, 467, 469, 471, 475
Hippeastrum
'Rilona', 251, 459
'Simply Red', 265, 461
'White Dazzler', 40, 439
Hippeastrum cybister
'Tarantula', 240, 459
Hyacinthus orientalis, 50, 91, 439, 443
'Delft Blue', 370, 471
Hydrangea macrophylla, 159, 285, 369, 380, 451, 463, 471, 473
'White Swan', 18, 437
Hylotelephium telephium, 324, 467

I

Iris germanica, 244, 459
'Black Knight', 383, 473
'Indian Chief', 346, 469
'Party Dress', 97, 445
Iris latifolia, 377, 473

J

Jasminum polyanthum, 86, 443

L

Lamprocapnos spectabilis, 311, 465
Lathyrus latifolius 'Albus', 60, 441
Lathyrus nervosus, 359, 471
Lathyrus odoratus, 58, 78, 135, 202, 242, 293, 298, 331, 347, 353, 441, 443, 447, 455, 459, 463, 465, 467, 469
'Matucana', 340, 469
Lavandula x intermedia, 368, 471
Leucojum aestivum, 59, 441
Leucospermum 'Carnival Orange', 215, 455
Liatris spicata, 343, 469
Lilium, 88, 107, 443, 445
'Orange Marmalade', 226, 457
'Premium Blond', 29, 437
'Solange', 204, 455
Lilium longiflorum, 171, 451
Lilium x dalhansonii, 395, 473
Limonium sinuatum, 98, 138, 310, 445, 449, 465
Lupinus x regalis, 354, 469
Lysimachia clethroides, 55, 439

M

Magnolia x soulangeana 'Alexandri-
na', 321, 467
Matricaria chamomilla, 169, 451
Matthiola incana, 22, 89, 101, 437,
443, 445
Muscari azureum 'Album', 54, 439
Muscari botryoides, 373, 471
Myosotis sylvatica, 371, 471

N

Narcissus
'Bridal Crown', 170, 451
'Johann Strauss', 212, 455
'Salome', 87, 443
'Soleil d'Or', 192, 453
'Tahiti', 178, 453
Narcissus papyraceus, 26, 437
Narcissus poeticus hybid, 48, 439
Narcissus pseudonarcissus,
193, 453
Nerine bowdenii 'Pallida', 32, 437
Nigella damascena, 68, 140, 441,
449
Nymphaea alba, 315, 465
Nymphaea nouchali, 362, 471

O

Oncidium 200, 455
hybrid 81, 189, 238, 239, 443,
453, 459
hybrid 'Kauai', 352, 469
Ornithogalum dubium, 218, 457

P

Paeonia
'Bowl of Cream', 39, 439
'Coral Charm', 300, 465
Paeonia lactiflora
'Black Panther', 387, 473
'Black Swan', 281, 463
'Chocolate Soldier', 282, 463
'Claire de Lune', 176, 453
'Day Star', 172, 451
'Dr Alexander Fleming', 305,
465
'Duchesse de Nemours', 79,
443
'Festiva Maxima', 70, 441
'Lady Gay', 123, 447
'Lemon Dream', 177, 453
'Nymphe', 313, 465
'Rooster Reveille', 77, 443
'Sarah Bernhardt', 318, 467
'Sonata', 76, 443
Paeonia x suffruticosa, 288, 463

'Burgundy Wine', 390, 473
'Callie's Memory', 249, 459
'Kopper Kettle', 111, 445
'Vesuvian', 385, 473
Papaver nudicaule, 220, 229, 255,
457, 459
Paphiopedilum, 174, 389, 451, 473
hybrid, 203, 455
Pericallis x hybrida, 361, 471
Phalaenopsis hybrid, 116, 447
Pieris japonica, 156, 451
Pimelea phylicoides, 74, 441
Polianthes tuberosa
'Pink Sapphire', 132, 447
'The Pearl', 149, 449
Polygonatum biflorum, 53, 439
Prunus glandulosa 'Sinensis',
133, 447
Prunus mume pink, 320, 467
Prunus x subhirtella 'Autumnalis',
20, 437

R

Ranunculus asiaticus 23, 114, 120,
152, 164, 186, 206, 214, 217,
261, 274, 280, 289, 299, 307,
344, 410, 437, 445, 447, 449,
451, 453, 455, 457, 461, 463,
465, 469, 475
'Butterfly Lux', 80, 443
'Charlotte', 243, 314, 459, 465
Clooney series 196, 222, 319,
455, 457, 467
Rhododendron molle hybrid, 16,
294, 437, 463
Rosa
'Amnesia', 128, 447
'Caffe Latte', 126, 447
'Cappuccino', 100, 445
'Combo', 205, 455
'Champagne', 84, 443
'Charity', 85, 443
'Distant Drum', 112, 445
'Emily', 108, 445
'Flash Night', 393, 473
'Garden Snow', 51, 439
'Golden Mustard', 167, 451
'Kahala', 250, 459
'Koko Loko', 161, 451
'Lady Moon', 306, 465
'Menta', 339, 469
'Pink Floyd', 297, 465
'Pink Majolica', 109, 445
'Pink Piano', 295, 463
'Pink Raddish', 124, 447
'Quicksand', 118, 447

'Red Piano', 276, 463
'Romantic Antike', 303, 465
'Royal Amethyst', 322, 467
'Sahara', 95, 443
'Sahara Sensation', 102, 445
'Secret Garden', 122, 447
'Tango', 115, 445
'Tibet', 27, 437
'Toffee', 234, 457
'White Majolica', 37, 439
Benjamin Britten 'Ausencart',
301, 465
Black Magic 'Tankalcig', 278,
463
Crocus Rose 'Ausquest', 175,
451
Juliet 'Ausjameson', 105, 445
Kate 'Auschris', 296, 465
Renaissance series 'Claire',
221, 457
Winchester Cathedral
'Auscat', 36, 439
Rudbeckia hirta 'Cherry Brandy',
404, 475

S

Sandersonia aurantiaca, 207, 455
Sarracenia leucophylla, 241, 459
Sarracenia x moorei, 400, 475
Scabiosa atropurpurea, 168, 384,
414, 451, 473, 475
Scabiosa caucasica, 137, 449
Scabiosa columbaria, 31, 317,
437, 467
Silene armeria, 335, 467
Solidago canadensis, 190, 453
Spiraea
'Arguta', 34, 437
Spiraea thunbergii , 75, 441
Strelitzia reginae, 213, 455
Syringa, 351, 469
Syringa vulgaris, 43, 439
'Beauty of Moscow', 131, 447

T

Tagetes patula, 198, 455
Telopea speciosissima, 302, 465
Tillandsia cyanea hybrid red
inflorescence, 266, 461
Trachymene coerulea 'Lacy Pink',
69, 441
Tulipa, 153, 187, 199, 308, 397, 449,
453, 455, 465, 475
'Apricot Beauty', 96, 445
'Black Hero', 279, 463
'Black Jack', 403, 475

'Blue Parrot', 341, 469
'Flaming Parrot', 227, 457
'Honeymoon', 63, 441
'Kingsblood', 263, 461
'Leo' , 232, 457
'Libretto Parrot', 117, 447
'Monte Spider', 184, 453
'Red Parrot', 270, 461
'Rococo', 394, 473
'White Liberstar', 49, 439
'White Parrot', 150, 449
'Yellow Flight', 182, 453
Tweedia caerulea, 375, 471
'Pint White', 19, 437

V

Veronica longifolia, 366, 471
Viburnum opulus 'Roseum', 151,
449
Viola hybrid 99, 181, 445, 453

X

Xerochrysum bracteatum, 283, 463

Z

Zantedeschia
'Aspen', 64, 441
'Black Star', 415, 475
'Kiwi Blush', 119, 447
'Mango', 225, 457
'Red Star', 401, 475
Zantedeschia aethiopica, 41, 439
Zinnia elegans, 253, 272, 459, 461
'Queen Lime Blush', 328, 396,
467, 475

Index of common names

A

Agapanthus, 139, 449
Allium, 28, 142, 155, 350, 374, 437,
    449, 469, 471
Amaryllis, 40, 240, 251, 265, 439,
    459, 461
Andromeda, 156, 451
Anemone, 33, 35, 273, 290, 323,
    363, 437, 461, 463, 467, 471
    Autumn anemone (also
    Japanese anemone), 325, 467
Anthurium, 65, 71, 224, 235, 248,
    268, 304, 336, 413, 441, 457,
    459, 461, 465, 469, 475
Astilbe, 61, 90, 284, 441, 443, 463
Astrantia, 42, 345, 439, 469
Autumn anemone, 325, 467
Azalea, 16, 294, 437, 463

B

Bearded iris, 97, 244, 346, 383,
    445, 459, 469, 473
Bell clematis, 357, 360, 471
Birds of paradise, 213, 455
Black Eyed Susan, 404, 475
Bleeding heart, 311, 465
Blue lace flower, 69, 441
Blue Star, 141, 449
Blue thistle, 378, 473
Boronia, 334, 467
Butterfly ranunculus, 80, 186, 206,
    261, 443, 453, 455, 461
Butterfly weed, 210, 455

C

Calendula, 195, 208, 453, 455
Calla lily, 41, 64, 119, 225, 401, 415,
    439, 441, 447, 457, 475
Campanula / bellflower, 136, 449
Carnation, 103, 125, 259, 402, 445,
    447, 461, 473, 475
    Spray carnation, 30, 38, 271,
    388, 437, 439, 461, 473
Celosia, 129, 447
Chamomile, 169, 451
Cherry blossom, 133, 447
    Flowering cherry, 20, 437
China aster, 367, 471
Christmas bush, 257, 461
Christmas rose, 158, 451
Chrysanthemum, 93, 173, 338, 443,
    451, 469
    Daisy mum, 173, 451

Spider mum, 233, 237, 457,
    459
Cineraria, 361, 471
Clematis, 355, 365, 469, 471
    Bell clematis, 357, 360, 471
Columbine, 382, 473
Cornflower, 376, 473
Cosmos, 67, 260, 392, 411, 441, 461,
    473, 475
Coxcomb, 127, 144, 201, 236, 275,
    447, 449, 455, 459, 461
Cyclamen, 17, 269, 437, 461
Cymbidium orchid, 286, 398,
    463, 475

D

Daffodil, 193, 453
Dahlia, 44, 66, 92, 104, 209, 228,
    245, 246, 247, 256, 258, 262,
    277, 291, 312, 333, 337, 407,
    439, 441, 443, 445, 455,
    457, 459, 461, 463, 465, 467,
    469, 475
Daisy mum, 173, 451
Delphinium, 342, 379, 469, 473
Dogwood, 82, 110, 443, 445

E

Easter lily, 171, 451
Echinacea, 316, 467
Epidendrum, 94, 216, 443, 457
Everlasting pea, 60, 441

F

Flannel flower, 24, 437
Floss flower, 364, 471
Flowering cherry, 20, 437
Forget-me-not, 371, 471
Forsythia, 180, 453
Foxglove, 83, 121, 330, 443, 447,
    467
Foxtail lily, 160, 451
Freesia, 47, 183, 439, 453
French marigold, 198, 455
French parrot tulip, 153, 227, 270,
    449, 457, 461
French tulip, 199, 263, 308, 455,
    461, 465
Fritillaria, 143, 145, 147, 219, 399,
    406, 449, 457, 475
    Snake's head fritillary, 165,
    451

G

Gerbera daisy, 57, 113, 185, 267, 326, 386, 441, 445, 453, 461, 467, 473
Ginger, 292, 463
Gladiolus, 45, 46, 62, 439, 441
Gloriosa lily, 179, 211, 453, 455
Golden lantern lily, 207, 455
Goldenrod, 190, 453
Gomphrena, 223, 457
Gooseneck loosestrife, 55, 439
Grevillea, 166, 329, 451, 467

H

Heath rice flower, 74, 441
Heather, 332, 467
Heliconia, 230, 264, 457, 461
Hellebore, 146, 148, 154, 158, 327, 349, 356, 412, 449, 451, 467, 469, 471, 475
Hyacinth, 50, 91, 370, 439, 443, 471
Hydrangea, 18, 159, 285, 369, 380, 437, 451, 463, 471, 473

I

Icelandic Poppy, 220, 229, 255, 457, 459
Iris, 377, 473
    Bearded iris, 97, 244, 346, 383, 445, 459, 469, 473

J

Japanese anemone 325, 467
James Story orchid, 239, 459
Jasmine, 86, 443

K

Kangaroo paw, 21, 163, 358, 437, 451, 471

L

Lady's slipper orchid, 174, 203, 389, 451, 455, 473
Larkspur, 25, 134, 372, 379, 381, 437, 447, 469, 471, 473
Lavender, 368, 471
Liatris, 343, 469
Lilac, 43, 131, 351, 439, 447, 469
Lily, 29, 88, 107, 204, 437, 443, 445, 455
    Calla lily, 41, 64, 119, 225, 401, 415, 439, 441, 447, 457, 475
    Easter lily, 171, 451
    Foxtail lily, 160, 451
    Gloriosa lily, 179, 211, 453, 455
    Lily of the valley, 52, 439
    Martagon hybrid, 226, 395, 457, 473
    Water lily, 362, 315, 465, 471
    Lily of the valley, 52, 439
Lisianthus, 56, 106, 287, 309, 348, 441, 445, 463, 465, 469
Lupine, 354, 469

M

Magnolia, 321, 467
Martagon hybrid, 226, 395, 457, 473
Mimosa, 191, 453
Muscari, 54, 373, 439, 471

N

Naples onion, 28, 437
Narcissus 48, 87, 170, 178, 192, 212, 408, 409, 439, 443, 451, 453, 455
Nerine, 32, 437
Nigella, 68, 140, 441, 449

O

Oncidium orchid, 81, 189, 200, 238, 352, 443, 453, 455, 459, 469
Orange chincherinchee, 218, 457
Orchid
    Cymbidium orchid, 286, 398, 463, 475
    Lady's slipper orchid, 174, 203, 389, 451, 455, 473
    James Story orchid, 239, 459
    Oncidium orchid, 81, 189, 200, 238, 352, 443, 453, 455, 459, 469
    Phalaenopsis orchid, 116, 447

P

Pansy, 99, 181, 445, 453
Paper white, 26, 437
Parrot tulip, 117, 341, 394, 447, 469, 473
Peony, 39, 70, 76, 77, 79, 123, 172, 176, 177, 281, 282, 288, 300, 305, 313, 318, 387, 390, 439, 441, 443, 447, 451, 453, 463, 465, 467, 473
Tree peony, 111, 249, 385, 445, 459, 473
Phalaenopsis orchid, 116, 447
Pincushion protea, 215, 455
Pitcher plant, 241, 400, 459, 475
Plum blossom, 320, 467
Plumosa celosia, 231, 391, 457, 473

Q

Queen Anne's lace, 157, 451
Quill, 266, 461
Quince, 72, 252, 254, 441, 459

R

Ranunculus, 23, 80, 114, 120, 152,
    196, 206, 214, 217, 222, 243,
    261, 274, 280, 289, 299, 307,
    314, 319, 344, 410, 437, 443,
    445, 447, 449, 455, 457, 459,
    461, 463, 465, 467, 469, 475
    Butterfly ranunculus, 186,
    453
    Ranunculus pom pom, 164,
    451
Rose, 27, 36, 37, 51, 84, 85, 95, 100,
    102, 105, 108, 109, 112, 115,
    118, 122, 124, 126, 128, 161, 167,
    175, 205, 221, 234, 250, 276,
    278, 295, 296, 297, 301, 303,
    306, 322, 339, 393, 437, 439,
    443, 445, 447, 451, 455, 457,
    459, 463, 465, 467, 469, 473

S

Scabiosa, 31, 137, 168, 317, 384, 414,
    437, 449, 451, 467, 473, 475
Sedum, 324, 467
Sicilian onion, 155, 449
Snake's head fritillary, 165, 451
Snowball viburnum, 151, 449
Snowflake, 59, 441
Solomon's seal, 53, 439
Spider mum, 233, 237, 457, 459
Spirea, 34, 75, 437, 441
Spray carnation, 30, 38, 271, 388,
    437, 439, 461, 473
Statice, 98, 138, 310, 445, 449, 465
Stock, 22, 89, 101, 437, 443, 445
Straw flower, 283, 463
Sunflower, 197, 405, 455, 475
Sweet pea, 58, 78, 135, 202, 242,
    293, 298, 331, 340, 347, 353,
    359, 441, 443, 447, 455, 459,
    463, 465, 467, 469, 471
    Everlasting pea, 60, 441
Sweet William catchfly, 335, 467

T

Tree peony, 111, 249, 385, 390, 445,
    459, 473
Tuberose, 132, 149, 447, 449
Tulip, 49, 63, 96, 117, 150, 153, 182,
    184, 232, 263, 279, 308, 397,
    403, 439, 441, 445, 447, 449,
    453, 457, 461, 463, 465, 475
    French parrot tulip, 153, 187,
    227, 270, 449, 453, 457, 461
    French tulip, 199, 455
    Parrot tulip, 341, 394, 469,
    473
Tweedia, 19, 375, 437, 471

V

Veronica, 366, 471

W

Waratah, 302, 465
Water lily, 362, 315, 465, 471
Wax flower, 73, 162, 441, 451
Witch hazel, 188, 453

Y

Yarrow, 130, 194, 447, 453

Z

Zinnia, 253, 272, 328, 396, 459, 461,
    467, 475

Phaidon Press Limited
2 Cooperage Yard
London E15 2QR

Phaidon Press Inc.
65 Bleecker Street
New York, NY 10012

phaidon.com

First published 2018
Reprinted 2019 (twice), 2021 (twice)
© 2018 Taylor Putnam and
Michael Putnam

ISBN 978 0 7148 7755 6 (US)
ISBN 978 0 7148 7830 0 (UK)

A CIP catalogue record for this book is
available from the British Library and
the Library of Congress.

Commissioning Editor: William Norwich
Project Editors: Ellen Christie and
        Rosie Pickles
Production Controller: Sarah Kramer

Designed by João Mota
Artwork by Albino Tavares

The authors would like to thank their
vendors on 28th Street in the New York
City flower market—without them, none
of this would be possible.

The publisher would like to thank
Jamie Compton for his help in
confirming the botanical names of
the flowers.

Printed in China